OH MY GOD, I'M GETTING OLDER
and So Is My Mom

SCOTT GREENBERG
SENIOR ADVOCATE & RADIO SHOW HOST

STAR
GROUP
BOOKS

Dedication

In the first edition of this book I highlighted how important a role my father-in-law, Leonard Weiss, played in inspiring us every day in our effort to improve the lives of the seniors we work with. That hasn't changed, although a lot else has since the first edition of this book was published. My daughter, Melissa, and her husband, Joe, have since joined the firm, helping Allison and Tino do what we do. My wife, Irene and I have a new grandchild, too, who brings us great joy! And our business has grown substantially since then as well.

Sadly, the need for this book and the message it sends has grown, too. More and more of us are aging and still have so many unanswered questions, not to mention misconceptions. While I have been unbelievably gratified by the response our first effort received, the need for this type of information, and the new information in the pages that follow, has never been greater. It is for that reason that I want to dedicate this book to all the family caregivers out there doing the best they can each and every day to improve the quality of life for their loved ones. You are the real heroes in this story and so...to you... THANK YOU FOR ALL YOU DO.

StarGroup International, Inc. West Palm Beach, Florida

Project Supervision: Brenda Star

Book design: Mel Abfier
Illustrator: Ray Russotto

Senior Editor: Gwen Carden
Associate Editor: Tracy Carvalho
Proofreaders: Carol Bassett, Tracy Carvalho

Designed and published by StarGroup Books

(561) 547-0667
www.stargroupinternational.com

Printed in Canada

Library of Congress Control Number: 2017957175

Oh My God, I'm Getting Older and So Is My Mom
ISBN 978-1-884886-42-3

Table of Contents

Preface

As Clerk and Comptroller, I often see families using the court system to try to help their aging friends or relatives get the resources they so desperately need. How did they get into this position? Why would they be asking a 3rd party to make life decisions when only a short time ago that decision making was taken for granted? I didn't fully understand the dynamics of the aging process until I read Scott Greenberg's book. "Oh My God, I'm Getting Older and So Is My Mom" is a rare, how-to, that is cleverly and humorously designed to offer practical guidance and advice for navigating the aging super-highway. Through Scott's experience and humor, we can begin a thoughtful, proactive plan for aging gracefully and with dignity.

The silver tsunami is here but it's hardly all doom and gloom! Scott's book gives us the tools to make intelligent decisions written in a common-sense format that is easy to follow. All mature readers, their children, caregivers and prospective caregivers will gain knowledge and a perspective suitable for sharing and empowering. Read it once, read it twice, then buy a copy to share with others. You will find the information is on target, timely and relevant.

Not only is Scott an entertaining author, but he is truly at the tip of a spear of a profound movement; a movement dedicated to the protection of the dignity and rights of incapacitated persons. Scott has been at the forefront of this movement. Through Scott's book, and his seminars, a national conversation has begun about the challenges of aging. But Scott also shows us opportunities, solutions and victories that are sure to come with a mature and seasoned society.

It has been my pleasure to get to know Scott through my Division of Inspector General Guardianship Investigation work. Scott exemplifies the many professionals who work hard at putting processes, procedures and laws in place to deal with the small fragment of society willing to exploit elders in guardianships. Through education and legal action we can and do hold people accountable for failure to provide quality services, respect and dignity to our aging communities.

Scott's book should be required reading for many segments of our society including but not limited to government and those serving the public. Thank you Scott for your meaningful work!

Sharon R Bock, Esq.
Clerk & Comptroller, Palm Beach County, Florida

Foreword

If there is one thing I know for sure it is that Scott Greenberg is no ordinary man.

His deep compassion and profound perspectives of this world afford him a unique glimpse into that stage of life—old age—which we all experience if we are lucky. Scott is also a man of profound integrity who does things because they are right, not because they are easy. In this book, he urges us to take control of our lives and make plans as carefully and with as much preparation and knowledge in this phase of life as we employed in our earlier years.

These short chapters offer deep insight, told in fable style, of how to avoid the potholes of our aging life. Through his sense of humor and inimitable style, Scott urges us to embrace our aging process by being prepared for what may come our way. I have learned much from Scott. He is a natural teacher to anyone open to hearing the lessons that have been meaningful in his life. He is a natural leader who is regularly sought out by professionals and "ordinary" folks as a resource, problem solver and trailblazer.

It is a great pleasure to write this foreword to Scott's book, as he is someone for whom I have the utmost respect and admiration. I have known Scott personally and professionally for six years and have had the privilege to present professionally with him at state and national conferences on nonprofit and business alliances and partnerships designed to offer client-centered, impactful services to older adults and their families.

I encourage you to savor these chapters and spend time digesting the imperative messages. Like kernels of popping corn, they might need to simmer awhile before taking shape.

Share this book with friends and family—anyone who might care about embracing a quality life.

Jenni Frumer, PhD, LCSW,MSEd, RG

Chief Executive Officer
Alpert Jewish Family & Children's Service
West Palm Beach, Florida

Introduction

In 2008 I was lucky enough to retire at age 58. All my dreams of carefree days at the golf course, world travel, and more time with grandchildren awaited. I had worked incredibly hard for over 20 years in the business I had just left, and I was really looking forward to every day being Sunday. Thinking I was financially secure and dreaming of the chance to do the things I always wanted to do but couldn't because of work commitments, I was fancy free and ready to enjoy the rest of my life.

And then reality hit. It was, after all, 2008 and the financial world was about to implode. Stocks tanked, real estate values crashed, interest rates began to fall and the income stream I depended on was about to be altered. Still, I had been a very conservative investor and planner and felt secure.

On Day One of my retirement, I got up, went to the gym at the club, and bumped into my friend, Larry. He greeted me with the following, "I heard you retired yesterday. So when is your urologist appointment?" I laughed, but not too hard, because indeed it was scheduled for the following week. Funny? Maybe. Prophetic? Sure seemed like it. Perhaps a sign of the future? Most definitely.

I spent the next 18 months living the dream. My wife, Irene, and I traveled with friends to Africa, spent many weeks in New York with our children and grandchildren and then took a bucket list trip to Vietnam. Of course, when the government wanted to send me there for free 40 years earlier I was less excited than I was this time around, but it was a terrific trip and much safer than it was in 1968. In between trips, I played golf five times a week, exercised like crazy, read books and newspapers, caught up on movies and watched my new reality set in. Sounds great doesn't it?

It wasn't.

I began to realize that doing nothing of substance left a big hole in who I was. I saw my friends at the golf course, usually older than I, begin to experience things they were not prepared for. Their money was running out; their investments couldn't support them. They were getting numerous ailments, friends and family started to die off and the conversations around the bagel table turned into a Groundhog Day event of complaining about politics, their golf game, the stock market, their ungrateful kids, their annoying and needy parents, and how they missed having a purpose and things to look forward to. These were typically fairly well-to-do folks who seemingly had the world by the short hairs, yet they were miserable—and making me miserable, too.

So I did what I always do when I get bored. I got busy again. Thinking that taking care of aging retirees in Florida might be a good business opportunity, I bought a home healthcare business. Boy was I smart, I thought. This would be a goldmine. Of course, 300 other clowns like me had the same thought, and so I entered a competitive, dog-eat-dog world I hadn't even known existed until then. You would think this world would be populated by unbelievably talented and caring people dedicated to improving the lives of seniors. Well, that was one more thing I was wrong about.

I discovered that many people who claim to be helping our seniors have agendas that tend to include separating them from their money to buy their product or service, whether it's good for them or not. I also discovered that seniors who found themselves at the mercy of this field were often completely unprepared for what lay ahead. I found people only addressing needs when in a crisis, enveloped in a scratchy wool blanket of confusion, family dysfunction, fear and distrust.

We are indeed living longer but not necessarily healthier, and we're running out of resources to live the dreams we've all cherished. For many, getting older is a nightmare—not just for Mom and Dad but for Baby Boomers and their kids, too. I began thinking about writing this book in 2010. Four years later the first edition was published. It was well-received by readers and also won two national book awards. After giving numerous talks about topics in the book and receiving feedback from readers, I decided in 2017 to update a few of the chapters and to add four more, as certain topics, like the changing face of health care, became more relevant.

Just as I told folks the first time around, the purpose of this book isn't to scare you or to sell any product or service. I simply want you to become aware, if you aren't already, that preparation and planning beat crisis management every day. You can, if you think through the things that are coming at you, be better able to navigate the waters ahead.

I've written some serious stuff in a lighthearted manner and hope you will read this and find some helpful hints to get you considering things you shouldn't overlook, long before you have no choices. For example, one chapter deals with funeral planning. Thinking about how you want to be buried isn't fun, but it needs to be addressed to make things easier on the loved ones you will leave behind. For me, I just want the doctors to be sure I'm dead.

I want you to take charge of important decisions ahead of time so when unscrupulous vultures descend, your family doesn't get victimized.

Don't wake up one day and say, "Oh My God, I'm Getting Older and So Is My Mom" and not know what to do. Just as hurricane preparation helps us weather the storms here in Florida where I live, this book will (hopefully) help you weather the inevitable storms of aging. Enjoy.

1

I'm OK, I Can Do It Myself

"Grandpa Scott, I can do it myself!" five-year-old Justin said as he struggled to tie his favorite little white Nike sneakers.

I tried to help him again.

"No, I'm OK. I can do it!" he insisted.

It took all I had not to squat down and do it for him, but I didn't. I knew that his struggle was part of the growing up process, and if he wanted help, he'd say so.

After a few tries Justin gave up, and before I could stop him he bounded into the other room, laces cascading over his foot like a plate of spilled spaghetti. A few seconds later I heard a "bump" and, on my watch, my adorable grandson had tripped on his laces and fallen, his head grazing the side of the couch. Fortunately he was OK, but I realized too late that a point had come when I should have stepped in and protected him from himself.

Working in the field that I do, it didn't take long before I made the connection between what had happened with Justin and what happens all the time in families with aging parents.

We ask them if they need help, and they say in no uncertain terms, "I can do it myself!" or "No, I'm fine." We worry a little, but in the end we believe them and go about our lives blissfully ignorant of the real situation. The next thing we know we get a call from the emergency room that mom or dad fell or got confused and took the wrong medication, or something else happened that easily could have been prevented.

"I'm fine" tells you no more about what's really going on than the typical "nothing" does when you ask a child what they learned in school that day.

It can mean it's no big deal (to them) that they've been eating only cereal because they can't carry heavy grocery bags anymore or that they're not bathing regularly because getting into and out of the tub or shower is just too difficult.

See where I'm going with this?

"I can do it myself!" is the battle cry of the proud Greatest Generation.

"I can do it myself!" is the battle cry of the proud Greatest Generation who lived through the Great Depression. Unfortunately, many of them are now engaged in the "Great Deception," especially where their children are concerned.

They feel that accepting help signals the end of their independence or makes them children again, when the truth is that accepting help where it's needed actually restores independence by giving them their quality of life back.

When Justin finally let me tie his shoes after his little fall, it didn't change a thing about who he was—he just now had safer shoes to go on with his day. It's no different when you help your parents—even ones who are stubborn.

I strongly believe that you should consider helping out your parent(s) if you believe they need it, even when they don't want any help. By framing your actions through the filter of the point of view I'm presenting here, you'll not only feel empowered to do what you have to do, but will also be able to explain it to your parent(s) in a way that will make sense to them.

In many cases parents are living in the "Land of Denial," or they will "fudge" the reality of what is going on. They don't want to worry you, after all. You have your own life and your own problems. You know that conversation. It's not supposed to "work that way." Parents take care of their children, not vice versa. (By the way, this is a very Western point of view. In many Asian cultures parents expect their children to care for them in their old age, and the children grow up knowing that that's the deal.)

In many cases parents are living in the "Land of Denial."

Western folks, however, consider asking their kids for help to be tantamount to tampering with who they are.

Well, here's an indisputable argument your parent can't ignore. When they call their doctor's office to make an appointment, does the doctor answer the phone? Of course not. That's what receptionists are for. When they arrive for their appointment, does the doctor take their vitals? No, again. Why? Because the doctor needs to spend his or her time taking care of what's really important—practicing medicine—and unapologetically enlists the help of medical assistants and other office personnel to do the more mundane tasks.

Just as the quality of the doctor's practice is enhanced by staff who helps, so is the quality of life of a parent who gets the help they need. It boils down to this: The issue shouldn't be about "leave me alone and let me die my own way," but

3

rather, what small changes can take place so that their quality of life gets better?

So, let's talk a little bit about what you're doing—or not doing—when you visit your aging parent(s).

If you're like many people, your visits are social. Mom or Dad say they're "fine," you make a little small talk, you fuss about something pertaining to their situation, and you leave.

Reality check: If you have any concerns whatsoever, it's time to pay attention and look for telltale signs that all is not well. Below are common places deficits show up.

Refrigerator
- Inspect the food. Is there too little (an indication they aren't eating regularly)?
- Is most of the food spoiled or expired?
- Does it contain nutritious food or a lot of junky, low nutrient food?

Hygiene
- How clean are their bed linens? Soiled linens could mean they don't have the energy or strength anymore to regularly change or wash the sheets.
- How clean are their clothes? If there is a large pile of dirty clothes or they are wearing clothes that obviously need to be washed, they may not be able to handle laundry anymore.
- Do you suspect they aren't bathing or washing their hair regularly? I've heard people tell me they don't shower daily because they "don't sweat."

Physical condition and outward appearances
- Are they gaining or losing a noticeable amount of weight?

- Are they getting their hair cut or styled regularly?
- Has your father stopped shaving?
- Has a parent who always dressed well stopped caring about the way they look?
- Are they not cutting their fingernails or toenails regularly?
- Can you tell they're not getting to the dentist regularly?

Social activity
- Has there been a drastic change in their social habits?
- Like my mother-in-law did, have they stopped or significantly cut down participation in their club or senior center?
- Are they still playing cards with friends?
- Have they stopped or significantly reduced how often they call or e-mail you?

You can, of course, expect a few changes with age, but when there are many of them or any of them is major, this is your cue to step in.

Take action, even if they fight you tooth and nail. It's easy to throw up your hands and say, "Mom won't let me help her." But do it anyway. Her life could depend on it.

Failing to get help can result in a poor quality of life for your parent. It pushes them into isolation, bad habits, dangerous decisions and habits that can endanger themselves and others.

There are things that are easy to do that can make a big difference without threatening their independence. For example:

- Hire someone to clean the house a couple of times a month. Make sure they do laundry and change the sheets.

- Find an organization that will deliver meals, such as Meals on Wheels. This serves two purposes: your parent will eat better, and someone will come to their home regularly.

- If no family member lives nearby, enlist a helper to take your parent out to do their errands and doctor visits. Non-medical home care agencies are everywhere. They can help with all activities of daily living. Don't be afraid to ask for a referral.

- Contact your local Area Agency on Aging, Elder Helpline or similar organization. Find out what resources are available in your community to help older people who need assistance.

What if you're lucky enough to still have both parents but know they need help, too? Don't be surprised if your father pushes back. He's been "the man of the family" for decades and is likely to think he's doing "just fine, thank you very much!"

Try to help your "stubborn" parent who wants to do it himself (or herself) understand that at some point, now or in the near future, it might be too much to continue doing without help. Explain that the stress could impact their health and thus how long they can continue doing the caregiving that they feel so strongly about doing.

Be patient, don't get discouraged. Familiarize yourself with the stages that I outline below—from obstinate rejection of help, to total acceptance—to help you gauge your progress and encourage you to continue to fight the fight:

Stage 1

"I don't want any help. I don't need any help. Leave me alone. I can do it myself."

Stage 2

"OK. I'll accept help if you insist, but I'm going to make everybody's life miserable."

Stage 3

"Hmm, having some help isn't so bad after all."

Stage 4

"How did I ever live without this?"

And finally, third parties can be a powerful weapon in your arsenal. If your parents won't listen to you, solicit the opinion of a trusted attorney, doctor or family friend. And, of course, get on the same page whenever possible with your siblings so you present a united front.

Third parties can be a powerful weapon in your arsenal.

2

"The Talk" (Not That Talk)

My wife, Irene, and I took one last look at each other, shrugged our shoulders in a "here-goes-nothing" sort of way, turned the key and walked in.

"Hi, Mom," Irene said, as her mother, Dinah, remained seated in her favorite worn-out blue fabric recliner.

"Hello, kids," my mother-in-law said with a big grin and then, with one long breath, added, "What took you so long? You're late. I thought you'd be here an hour ago."

Irene and I had just flown in from our home in South Florida for a visit with Dinah, who lived in a modest two-bedroom co-op apartment in Queens, New York. We wanted to check up on her to be sure she was doing OK, but the truth was we had another agenda. And it wasn't the first time we'd had that agenda.

Once an active person who went to the senior center three times a week and often played cards, Dinah, now widowed, was becoming isolated. Many of her friends had died or moved to Florida; her life consisted mostly of knitting, watching TV and doing crossword puzzles. Even her visits to the senior center had decreased to less than once a week. Her 10-year-old gray Ford Taurus with 5,000 miles on it and matching dents on all four fenders sat unused and deteriorating. We joked that Mom made periodic trips to the hospital just to meet new people to talk to.

All joking aside, we had become increasingly concerned that she might fall one day and not be discovered for hours—or worse.

After exchanging some pleasantries, I cleared my throat and braced myself for what I knew was coming. Despite lacking confidence in a good outcome, I began my speech.

"Mom, Irene and I are very worried about you. We don't think you should be alone anymore. We believe you need to......"

"I am not going to a home!"

"I.....am.....not.....going.....to.....a.....home!" she interrupted. "I am going to stay here until I die."

Ummm, now what? Here we go again.

Then came the begging (ours). And the pleading (ours). And maybe even a little bit of guilt thrown in from us for good measure but, alas, nothing worked.

Once again we were vanquished by a little old gray-haired lady in 1950s elastic pants and an oversized will to match the oversized blouse she wore.

"What are you gonna do?" I asked rhetorically to Irene in exasperation as we headed back for the airport. Oh, well.

In retrospect, I understand now that even though Dinah's environment didn't support her quality of life, she had no way of knowing that a different living situation would have in fact given her more independence, not taken it away. Framing the situation this way would have created a whole different feel for all of us. But we didn't know that then. There was so much we didn't know.

Five years later Dinah did fall. She broke her hip while trying to step up into a bus, and while she didn't lie undiscovered in her apartment, she never recovered from her fall. Following surgery, she languished in the hospital for two weeks and then died from complications. I believe that our inability to convince Dinah to agree to an alternative living arrangement led indirectly to her death. While she still could have fallen, she probably would not have had she been in an environment built specifically to support people who are aging. And frankly, I don't feel very good about that.

We were ill-equipped to talk to my mother-in-law in a way that would have helped her see things differently. I only wish I had known then what I know now.

OK, so, let's get real here.

Nobody wants to be on either end of the "old folks home" conversation any more than they want to be on either end of the "birds and the bees" conversation between parents and adolescents. But this is an essential conversation for millions of Baby Boomers these days who are concerned with aging parents. The sooner the better in a lot of cases.

As with my mother-in-law, most elderly people consider going to "a home" to be a defeat. Mom would say, "I don't want to be one of those old people."

You have to get started sometime, so here's what you can do.

Start by evaluating how much local support your parent has. Do you or a sibling live close enough that you can take your parent to the doctor and the supermarket and check in on them regularly? If not, the stakes of letting your parent remain "independent" get higher.

When the time comes to have "the talk," get out of your own head and make the discussion about them, not you. What I mean is, don't make them feel like *they* need to change just so you will feel better. Don't try to make them feel guilty for not doing what you think they should do.

Instead, come armed with plenty of non-emotionally-charged ammunition. Here are a few things to consider:

- Talk to your parent about their safety and health. "Mom, I am concerned that you could fall and no one would be here to call for help." Expect denial. "Oh, I'm not going to fall." You and I know that's most likely not the case.

- Know what type of community is appropriate for your parent at his or her stage of independence so you can make some recommendations (see explanation of various options below). Visit senior living communities in your target area.

- Learn about costs. What sorts of activities do they have? What requirements need to be met to become a resident? Are there special accommodations available? Take brochures and videos of the community to show your parent. Research the options on the internet.

- Try to get your parent interested in a community where he or she already has friends. One of Dinah's biggest fears was going someplace where she wouldn't know anyone. Many of Dinah's friends were in residential communities in Florida, and I think Dinah would have thrived had she been able to reunite with them. We could have enlisted those friends as allies but didn't think about doing that.

Make the discussion about them, not you.

- Involve your siblings or even your children in helping convince your parent that making a move is in their best interest. The more people who care about your parent that get involved in the process, the more likely it is to succeed.

- Avoid scare tactics. Logic can be more convincing than hysteria.

- Be firm. Just because your parent pushes back doesn't mean you should give up. Keep at it. Be relentless if you must. I wish we hadn't given up.

Now it's time to talk about options. First of all, not all "nursing homes" are true nursing homes. "Nursing home" has become a generic term that has a repugnant, stereotypical reputation as a smelly place with people staring blankly out into space from their wheelchairs. To put it simply, today's options are much better than your grandmother's nursing home.

Not all "nursing homes" are true nursing homes.

Let's instead refer to the variety of choices as "long-term care options."

Here is a brief description of the types.

Independent Living

Independent living is like hotel living. It is typically set up as a community for people who do not need assistance with daily activities like cooking or dressing, and while age restrictions vary by state, 75-85 is the average age. Residents frequently occupy small houses or apartments and may have access to meals, basic housekeeping, laundry services and transportation. Independent living communities cost $2,000-$4,000 per month depending on what services are needed and where it's located.

Assisted Living
Assisted living is similar to independent living but is the next stage. Residents tend to have some level of disability and are monitored for their health and safety. Assisted living provides assistance with activities of daily living such as medication management and bathing, and provides full meal service. Assisted living can range from $3,000-$6,000 per month based on level of care and geographical location.

Memory Care
Memory care-specific assisted living communities are for people with dementia. It allows them to be closely monitored while providing appropriate freedom and activities. They are often found within assisted living facilities or nursing homes, or can be self-contained individual homes within a community. Typical cost ranges from $5,000-$7,000 per month.

CCRC (Continuing Care Retirement Communities)
CCRCs are retirement communities offering several levels of care onsite: independent living, assisted living, and skilled nursing care (the conventional "nursing home" level of care). Some may offer memory care (for people with dementia). The advantage of these communities is that, should their needs change, the resident does not have to relocate. Should a couple reside there and each requires a different level of care, they are still able to remain near one another. In many cases you "buy into" these communities and thus have some equity in them, but that option is typically very expensive.

Nursing Home

As hard as it is for us to imagine, 85% of us will be a patient in a skilled nursing facility at some point in our lives, for rehab or some other reason. A nursing home is for people who are unable to care for themselves and need continual nursing care. While the majority of residents are elderly, nursing homes care for people of all ages who are ill or who have had an accident and need intensive nursing care in order to resume life in the general population. Nursing home costs average around $10,000 per month but can be less or more. Medicare provides nursing home, or more accurately, skilled nursing coverage, for a maximum of 100 days, the last 80 of which require a significant co-pay. Medicaid coverage is available in most states for people who qualify.

We know that nobody wants to go into long-term care, and most people think they'll never end up there. Heck, I'd like to die on the golf course after just having had a hole in one.

But the fact is that a large percentage of the population will, in fact, need that sort of service during their lifetime, and for that reason I strongly recommend you be proactive. Finding the right option for a parent is no simple matter, and trying to do so in the midst of a crisis simply doesn't make sense.

Just remember, you aren't "parking your parent" until they die. You're just doing for them what they did for you. Taking care of them.

You aren't just "parking your parent" until they die.

15

3

Use My Doctor. He's The Best!

If you're not retired yet, you're probably fantasizing about it. Sunny days on the golf course. Lazy afternoons reading on the beach. Visits with the grandkids. Shopping at the mall during low traffic times. Champagne toasts at sunset. Sleeping in.

Problem is, there's something big missing in most lists. At least it was in mine. It involves visits to all those "ologists." You know, the ones who poke and prod you and sometimes give you bad news.

Here is a story about what happened to me on the very first day of my new retirement from my last career that brought "ologists" stampeding onto the top of my whimsical list of retirement activities.

I was 58 years old and asking myself, "What the hell do I do now?" Well, why not use my newfound extra time to get into better shape? It was the first morning that I didn't have to pay attention to the alarm clock, but I awoke early (anyway) and went to the fitness center at my golf club. A good friend of mine greeted me with, "Hey, Scott, I heard you retired yesterday. So, when is your urologist appointment?"

"So, when is your urologist appointment?"

We laughed, but I really didn't laugh that much. I actually *did* have an appointment the following week to see my urologist. Had I turned into a geezer stereotype in less than 24 hours?

It dawned on me that as we age we get introduced to one ologist after the other. There are ur**ologists** for that very special part of our anatomy, dermat**ologists** for our skin conditions and ophthalm**ologists** for our declining eyesight...well, you get the picture. I don't know about you, but I'm meeting more people with big titles after their name and multiple diplomas on their wall than I ever wanted to.

I visit my gastroenter**ologist** for a regularly scheduled meeting. Of course the meeting I'm talking about is a pair of rubber tubes going in from both ends until they meet in the middle. At that point, the meeting is over.

From there I go to the cardi**ologist** to make sure the ticker is going to keep on ticking. How about the hemat**ologist** for my blood work? Can't forget that, can we? And then what if, God forbid, we have a scare?

Now we sit on pins and needles waiting for the path**ologist's** report. If it's bad news, we get introduced to onc**ologists**; and then to psych**ologists** to manage our emotions so we can begin to deal with what lies ahead.

Oy vey, what happened to my dreams of moonlit nights on the beach with a glass of wine and the wind blowing through my hair (no hair jokes, please) and the endless rounds of great golf that I thought retirement was all about?

I don't know about you, but I don't want to talk to these medical ologists anymore. I only want to talk to people like geologists, archeologists and other ologists who can teach me how we all got here or how the beautiful sights I see on my long-planned vacations were formed.

Actually, though, there is one ologist I really do want to have more time with—my mix**ologist**. Now he's one ologist I love seeing on a regular basis even though all the other ologists say he's no good for me. What do they know anyway?

OK, we really can't avoid the ologists (also known as doctors), but we can decide which one(s) are right for us. And that might not be just because your friend said so.

Let me ask you a question: Have you ever heard anyone say, "Go to my doctor. He's second best?" Of course not. Everyone thinks their doctor is "the best," but based on what? That's where the work on your part comes in.

You might be surprised to learn this, but outcomes rarely have anything to do with how smart our doctors are, although it helps not to have a dumb doctor. What matters is how caring they are, how familiar they are with you, how willing they are to stop and listen, and most importantly, how in touch they are with your view of what a good outcome for you will be so that they know what is in your best interest.

We all have had doctors, lawyers, accountants, stockbrokers, teachers and others who, in some way, influenced our lives. Were the best outcomes always from the smartest men or women in the room? More often the best outcomes came when you clearly expressed your needs, your goals, and what you were most interested in accomplishing.

My internist tells me that he is often asked what the best hospital in the area is. His answer? "The one closest to you when you need it." In other words, the doctor you choose needs to be the right one for you, not the right one for your friend.

It amuses me when I hear my friends say that "All the good

"All the good doctors are in New York."

doctors are in New York." It makes me think that knowing how to shovel snow is a prerequisite for being a competent physician. That is just plain silly. If you have a life-threatening condition, you may want to seek out the country's foremost authority on it, but that person could be in Seattle, Chicago or Valdosta. If your need is for a primary physician or one treating a non-life-threatening illness, look closer to home.

Ask your friends for a recommendation, then do your homework. Just because one "best doctor" is a proficient cardiologist doesn't mean he or she should replace your heart valve.

These are the factors I always take into consideration when choosing my ologists (and believe me, I've had plenty of them since I retired for the first time in 2008). P.S. You might have to "shop" a few doctors to find one who meets these criteria:

- Board certification in the appropriate specialty.

- Relevancy: are they using the latest knowledge and technology or still stuck in the last century?

- Personality—do you actually *like* them? Doctor-patient communication is enhanced when this sort of synergy exists.

- Willingness to take time to listen to you and minimize the amount of time he or she spends looking at the computer filling out your electronic medical record. (See Chapter 18 for more about electronic medical records.)

- Number of patients they treat with your specific condition, in their particular specialty; or, in the case of surgery, a high number of that specific surgery performed annually.

- Legal status. Have they had a lot of lawsuits filed against them? You can usually find this out on state professional licensing websites. (One lawsuit might not concern me that much, depending on what it was. Several would be a red flag.)

We Baby Boomers were taught as children that doctors are "gods." Get over that. Now. They are human beings who have good days and bad days, personal problems and concerns, just like the rest of us.

Doing your homework is important because...guess what they call the person who graduated last in their class at medical school?

Doctor!

The burden of great outcomes depends on you. You must not be a shrinking violet in all things important to you. Step up and shout until you're heard. And if the professional you've chosen can't rise to the occasion, fire them and find another one who will.

Oh, and by the way, I actually did go once to the second best doctor in a specialty I needed, and he really screwed up my shoulder. I've never been the same. Maybe he didn't hear me when I said I wanted to play racquetball again. And I thought he was a good listener.

4

We Take Too Many Damn Drugs

Let me set something straight. I'm not anti-doctor and I'm not anti-drug (the legal stuff, of course), but I do worry about how widespread prescription drug use is and how ignorant we often are about using prescribed medications.

Recently I was having dinner with five friends at my country club when, right before ordering, three of them pulled out either a pill bottle or box and gulped down God-only-knows-what, without ever missing a beat in the conversation. Two were women, and I noticed them discreetly eyeing each other's ornate pill boxes (the pill popping man was oblivious); I concluded that they were silently assessing who had the more elegant case. I was intrigued that this little ritual was so ingrained among the diners that no one (except me, of course) seemed to think anything of it—beyond the unspoken fashion competition.

Yes, it got me thinking (again) about something I knew I wanted to cover in this book. I guess you could call it the "responsible way to do drugs."

If you're a Baby Boomer in good health you may not be taking a lot of medications, but your parents probably are... and they may not be managing those medications very well.

Only 47% of medications are taken properly by people released from the hospital.

One statistic I saw stated that, on average, Medicare patients who are being discharged from the hospital go home tasked with taking 13—yes, 13—prescription medications. Most likely those 13 aren't prescribed by just one physician, so you can bet that all parties involved don't know the full medication list. With so many instructions for the patient to understand and follow, it's not surprising that another study reported that just 47% of medications are taken properly by people released from the hospital.

How likely would you be to comply with 13 sets of instructions? I have trouble reading just one set of directions on how to open some of those "hermetically sealed" envelopes that arrive in the mail every week.

When multiple doctors are ordering prescriptions, who is there to make sure there are no dangerous interactions taking place?

You can't count on your doctor or the nurse to do this. They may not be aware of every single medication you're taking, or they may be very busy and don't think about it or they just give you a cursory opinion.

To be safe, this is where your pharmacist comes in. I think pharmacists are an underutilized resource. They will, for free, tell you everything you need to know about your medications. In certain situations, that service could help save your health and maybe even your life.

So let's have a chat about safely medicating.

If you or your parents are taking several medications, it's time to make a field trip to the drug store, no permission slip required. Place everything in a bag (including non-prescription medications, vitamins and supplements), walk up to the counter and ask the pharmacist to do a "medication reconciliation." This process is designed to determine if there are potential dangerous interactions among the medications or if there is additional information available to help those medications be consumed safely or more effectively.

We've had clients of our agency who were taking Lipitor in the morning and Crestor in the afternoon. These are both statin drugs and there would never, ever, be a reason to take both at the same time.

Years ago I remember looking inside my mother's medicine cabinet and discovering—to my horror—that she had pills in their original bottles dating back 10 years!

"Why do you still have these?" I asked her. "Scott, you never know when you might need them."

Oh, boy. Not only was she putting herself at risk by being her own prescribing physician, but anything she took would be way beyond expired, more like prehistoric. Out they went. She was not amused. Too bad, Mom.

So, let's have a little chat about safely medicating. It won't be as interesting as a chat about safe sex, but it can be just as important for your health.

Follow and understand the directions
This sounds like it's a joke, but researcher Dr. Michael Wolf at Chicago's Feinberg School of Medicine reported reading about a patient's confusion in a pharmacist's log from the 1890s, housed at the Smithsonian National Museum of American History. When instructed to "Shake well," the patient asked, "Does that mean I shake myself?"

A lot of time has passed since that log entry was made, but people still get confused about how to comply with medication instructions. According to Wolf's published study, the more medications a patient takes, the more likely he or she is to misinterpret the directions.

Here are some examples that can be open to interpretation. I'm sure you've encountered these more than once.

Take two pills twice a day
Does this literally mean every 12 hours, or can you take them twice during your waking hours?
Do you take two pills each time or one pill two times?

Take every six hours
Does this mean you need to wake yourself up during the night or can you go eight hours between two of the doses?

Take on an empty stomach
How do you know if your stomach is empty?
How many hours before or after a meal can you take it?

Do not operate machinery while taking this drug
Does that mean you can't drive?

If there is any doubt whatsoever about what the instructions mean, find out from the doctor or pharmacist—and be careful.

Not long ago I had been taking two Tylenol every four hours for some back pain and decided to try Motrin. I didn't bother to read the label before downing two Motrin and bounding out the door. Later that day when I got home and slowed down enough to catch my breath, I read the label and discovered a goof. You only take one Motrin at a time. It's not the same medication. Never assume.

And finally, do not get the mindset that if one is good, two are better. Directions are there for a reason. Don't think you know better than the professional who wrote them.

Avoid taking other people's medications

I will start by tattling on myself with an admonishment to "Do as I say, not as I do."

One day while at the golf course, I commented to a friend that I was experiencing shoulder pain. He said, "Here, take a couple of my muscle relaxers."

Being the guru of good sense and a bastion of intelligent advice-giving, guess what I did. I said, "Thanks, Jim," and gulped one down, sticking the other in my pocket for later.

Luckily I lived to tell about it, but I knew in the back of my mind that I was putting myself at risk. I happen to know that the type of medication doctors typically prescribe for toenail fungus can damage my liver because I have high liver enzymes. I'd never take that medication; but I had no idea if any underlying condition of mine might have been exacerbated by a muscle relaxant. I could have endangered myself, so don't do what I did. It's not worth the risk.

"Here, take a couple of my muscle relaxers."

Don't assume that over-the-counter medications are harmless

A lot of people don't realize that taking too much Tylenol can cause serious liver damage. (NOTE: please reference the warning label on the packaging.) Just because you don't need a prescription for a medication doesn't mean it's harmless. All medications (and even supplements like vitamins) can be harmful if taken inappropriately. Don't be your own doctor.

Make sure you are able to identify possible side effects and that you know what to do about them

Some side effects are "mild" and go away. Others are a signal that the drug is wrong for you and require a call or visit to the doctor. Learn in advance what to look for.

Tell your doctor everything about your medications
Even if it's vitamins and supplements, the doctor needs to know. The best thing you can do is give the doctor a list of all your medications, dosages and instructions. Bring the bottles along at the time of your visit for verification.

You don't get a pass on this advice just because electronic medical records are becoming more the norm. They're not foolproof. Especially not yet. First, they may not have notations about over-the-counter medications you are taking. There can be human error, not all your records may have been entered yet; and if you order any of your medications from a foreign pharmacy, they won't show up.

Oh, and back to taking too many damn drugs.

As sophisticated as you are, remember that pharmaceutical companies advertise heavily to the general public in order to worry you that you might have a certain illness or condition and prompt you to go see your doctor and ask for their product. Think depression, "low T," impotence and a host of other ailments.

While I'm not a doctor, I would think twice about running to the doctor every time I sneeze, demanding a prescription cure. The vast majority of minor illnesses clear up on their own. Unless you are experiencing severe pain or a disturbing symptom like fainting, shortness of breath or chest pain (or anything else a prudent person would figure out is way beyond normal), give it a while. Many doctors feel compelled to write a prescription, even if you don't need it, and that's contributing, in my opinion, to Americans taking too many damn drugs.

5

80 In The Left Lane Going 20

My best friend, Marty, still cringes when he remembers the night in 2011 when his father picked him up from the Fort Lauderdale airport and drove 30 miles on I-95 to his condo in Boynton Beach.

Here's how he describes it:

"Pop cautiously entered the freeway going 20 mph with no concern for the fact that the cars in that lane were going 55. The guy right behind us had to slam on his brakes to keep from hitting us, and when he went around, he showed us with a creative gesture just how much he appreciated our contribution to the enjoyment of his journey. Pop stayed in the right lane for a while (sort of) before drifting into the far left lane with a mere glance in his rearview mirror. He remained in the left lane most of the way to Boynton Beach at the breakneck speed of 45 while frustrated and rushed drivers ping-ponged around him. He missed the exit, and we nearly got rear-ended when he suddenly crossed two lanes and slammed on his brakes in a valiant, yet failed, effort to correct his course. By then I was drenched and swimming in a puddle of sweat. After getting off at the next exit unevent-fully, I convinced him not to get back on the freeway, and we took the slow way to his house. While we waited at a traffic

He parked three-fifths of his car in one spot and two-fifths in the spot next to it.

light he said, 'I sure don't see as well at night as I used to.' You think?! He pulled into the parking lot at his complex, parked three-fifths of the car in one parking spot and two-fifths in the one next to it, and turned off the ignition. I opened the trunk to get my luggage, walked through my father's front door, set my bag down, turned to my father and said, 'Pop, give me the keys. You are never driving again.'"

Can you guess how Marty's father responded?

If you answered "not well," you win the seven-day all-expense-paid vacation to Hawaii. Of course it didn't go well, for several reasons.

First, Marty's father's manhood was attached to those car keys, and he wasn't going to give them up without a fight. Also, Marty hadn't thought out well—or at all, really—how to broach the subject so his father wouldn't be defensive. Marty spoke impulsively because he was still getting over nearly being killed six times in 45 minutes. Marty didn't give his father any reason for the demand (you can't assume his father knew how badly he was driving), nor did he offer him any solutions. Oh, and Marty's father, a widower, was a hot commodity at his condo and was still driving at night (though he shouldn't have been), squiring all the widows around to early bird specials and bingo games.

When you're an elderly man who drives at night you are the ultimate catch regardless of what you look like. It's "Come on down! The price is right!"

Without a doubt, the "keys" discussion is one of the most difficult.

You really can't blame Marty for the way he handled the situation. After all, there's no instruction manual for what to do when you believe your parent needs to stop driving. Without a doubt, the "keys" discussion is one of the most difficult ones you will have with your aging parent.

If your loved one has been diagnosed with cognitive impairment, you must take the keys away. You are tempting fate if you don't.

Your loved one can also end up in jail if they are driving erratically or dangerously. Typically police officers are not trained to deal with people with cognitive impairment. Don't let this happen.

If your loved one has been diagnosed with cognitive impairment, you must take the keys away. You are tempting fate if you don't.

6

What The Hell Is An ADL?

Understanding Your Long-Term Care Insurance

After rapping loudly on the door I walked into Louise's condo. I had stopped by in response to a call from her daughter who was concerned that Louise, who was hard of hearing, had reached a point of needing some extra help taking care of herself. Louise wasn't bathing regularly anymore, and she was losing control of her bladder more and more often.

Louise and I had spoken on the phone, so she was expecting me. Looking up from her newspaper, she said with a serious expression, "You must be Scott."

"I am," I responded, carefully yelling as quietly as possible—if it's possible to yell quietly—so as not to sound unfriendly. "And you must be Louise. How are you, Louise?"

"Just fine," she replied, as she set her newspaper down on an enormous pile of other newspapers that must have been living in that spot since 1992.

"Louise," I added sternly. "You are not fine, and this has to be the last time you ever say that."

She looked at me like I was speaking Martian. I had expected that.

"Why can't I ever say that again?" she asked with both curiosity and irritation in her voice. She wasn't all that thrilled to have finally acknowledged that she needed assistance from an agency, and speaking nonsense to her didn't help things.

You are not "fine." "Because," I responded, "if you're 'fine,' your long-term care insurance won't pay for you to get the help you need to make your life around here a little easier."

Fortunately for Louise, she and her late husband Phillip had taken out long-term care insurance, and now that Louise was having trouble with some "activities of daily living," it was time to take advantage of it. Getting the most out of her insurance required being honest about her condition so that all the pieces would fall neatly into place—and that meant not saying she was "fine" when she wasn't.

What exactly is long-term care insurance?

Long-term care insurance is insurance that helps pay for long-term care in your home (or in some cases and states, in independent or assisted living communities) should you become temporarily or permanently ill or unable to perform necessary health-related activities. This care can be medical in nature, such as nursing visits, but is more often for non-medical needs such as bathing and toileting.

Although policies are all different, in most cases to receive benefits the patient must be unable to independently accomplish a minimum of two of five or six common "activities of daily living" (ADLs). These include: bathing, dressing, eating, toileting, continence and transferring (getting from place to place such as from the bed to the bathroom).

According to the U.S. Department of Health and Human Services, nine million Americans over the age of 65 currently need long-term care. That statistic is predicted to catapult to 12 million by the year 2020, and most will be cared for at home by family and friends.

Caring for a loved one can be debilitating, and here's a scary fact: 64% of family caregivers will pre-decease a loved one they're caring for who has dementia if they don't get outside help.

64% of family caregivers will pre-decease a loved one who has dementia if they don't get outside help.

Buying long-term care insurance makes it possible for the caregiver to have access to the kind of respite care that will improve the quality of their life—and quite possibly extend it. It also ensures that the patient will get help sooner, because somebody else is paying for it, which can help lengthen the life of your loved one.

Whaaatt??? Doesn't Medicare or Medicaid pay for this?
No, it doesn't, although there are state-specific exceptions for Medicaid (check your state regulations). And that's a common misconception. So let's get down to business.

I'm writing this chapter with both you, the Baby Boomer, and your parent in mind.

Let's start with Mom and Dad.

First of all, do you know if your parents have long-term care insurance?

If they have it, do you know what it does and doesn't cover, when it kicks in and if it's paid up and current?

If you can't answer those questions, you need to get the answers. Today would be a good time to do it. Yesterday would be even better.

I can't tell you how often I speak with the children of our clients who have only a vague idea that there might be such a policy in existence, but they aren't sure and don't know where to start looking for it. Don't wait until there's a crisis before finding this out. Being ignorant could cost the family thousands of dollars, especially in the case of a chronic illness. Full-time custodial care can cost as much as $80,000 a year or more. If your parents paid for long-term care and need it, use it!

Now let's talk about you.

Should you buy long-term care insurance?

For most people, the answer is "yes" for the reasons I talked about above, but it's not appropriate for everyone.

There's about a 70% chance you'll need some type of long-term care after age 65.

The reason I say "yes" for most people is that the odds are not in your favor. According to the non-profit LIFE Foundation (www.lifehappens.org) there's about a 70% chance you'll need some type of long-term care after age 65.

Unfortunately, not everyone can afford long-term care insurance, because it is expensive. Like all other insurance, the younger you are when you buy it, the cheaper it is.

Long-term care insurance doesn't make sense for people with significant means who could easily spend $80,000 a year and not miss it. It's not likely to be a priority, either, for people with lavish lifestyles including travel and expensive cars. Those luxuries would go away in the face of a serious illness, and the funds could then be diverted to long-term care.

Like everything else...be a good consumer

Like everything else you spend money on, you need to be a good consumer. Do your homework. I always advise people to "*buy* insurance, not *be sold* insurance."

Before buying, here is an informative list of things to know and do, offered by the Texas Long-Term Care Partnership:

- Although it may be difficult, try to anticipate what services you might need in the future and choose a policy that's right for you. Creating your plan prior to shopping will help you identify and better understand your needs.

- Prices can vary substantially from one company to another, even for policies with similar benefits. Get quotes from several companies before buying a policy. A company's financial rating by an independent rating service is a helpful indication of the company's overall financial strength.

- The number of consumer complaints against a company is a good indication of the company's customer service record. Your family and friends can be a great source of information about a company's customer service, so be sure to ask them if they've had any experience with the companies you're considering.

- Licensed companies belong to a guaranty association that will pay your claim if your insurance company goes broke. If you buy from an unlicensed company and have a claim, it might go unpaid.

- While past increases are not a guarantee or predictor of future increases, you may want to take the rate history into consideration.

- If you buy insurance through the mail or by phone, ask whether the company has a local agent or a toll-free number you can call if you have questions.

- Because of the many variations in long-term care policies, having an agent with knowledge and experience can help you choose the right coverage for your needs.

- Find out if the insurance company must give you at least 30 days to look over your long-term care policy after you receive it. Read the policy carefully to be sure it has the benefits and features you want. If you decide to return the policy within the 30 days, you will get a full refund of any premium paid, if this law is in effect in your state. It's a good idea to use certified mail so you will have proof that you returned the policy. Be sure to keep a copy of everything you return.

Before making a decision on any one particular policy, be sure you understand all the terms and conditions. Below is a short primer, courtesy of LIFE, on what you absolutely must know in order to understand what you are getting:

Benefit Amount and Duration
Most long-term care policies are set up as indemnity plans, which means they pay a fixed dollar amount for each day you receive care. Policyholders usually have a choice of daily benefit amounts ranging from $50 to $300 or more, and can also choose the length of time that benefits will be paid. Long-term care policies generally limit benefits to a maximum dollar amount or a maximum number of days and may have separate benefit limits for nursing home, assisted living community, and home health care within the same policy. For example, a policy may offer $100 per day up to five years of nursing home coverage (many policies now offer lifetime nursing home coverage) and only up to $80 per day up to five years of assisted living and home health care coverage.

Elimination or Deductible Periods

These terms refer to how many days you must pay out-of-pocket for services that would otherwise be covered before benefits kick in. Most policies offer a choice of deductible from zero to 100 days. The longer the elimination or deductible period, the lower the premium.

Exclusions

When you apply for a policy, you'll be asked to fill out a medical questionnaire, and probably undergo a checkup with a doctor. This helps the insurance company find out about any existing health issues (known as preexisting conditions) that make it more likely that you'll one day need long-term care. Preexisting conditions may make coverage more expensive, and the insurance company may choose not to cover you for these conditions during your first six months of coverage.

Inflation Protection

Because long-term care prices are rising steadily, the benefit you buy today may be inadequate tomorrow. By purchasing inflation protection, your policy benefit will automatically increase each year at a specified rate (such as five percent) compounded over the life of the policy.

Non-forfeiture Benefits

This feature allows you to drop your coverage and still receive a portion of the benefits. Non-forfeiture benefits may be received two ways, depending on the policy and option you choose. Return of premium provides a cash payment that is a percentage of the total premiums you have paid. With a shortened benefit period, you still receive coverage after you've stopped paying, but with a reduced benefit period or amount.

Renewability

Almost all long-term care policies are guaranteed renewable.

That means that they cannot be canceled as long as you pay your premiums. However, companies can raise premiums as long as they raise them for an entire class of policyholders. The renewability provision, usually found on the first page of the policy, outlines under what conditions the company can cancel the policy or raise premiums.

Waiver of Premium
This provision allows you to stop paying premiums while you are receiving benefits. Your policy may contain restrictions on this feature, such as requiring you to receive care for a certain number of days or sessions before premiums are waived.

But wait. There's more (that you need to know)!

To get long-term care benefits, you have to have a care plan prepared by a nurse or social worker. Often the doctor has to state that the patient needs help with activities of daily living (ADLs).

Some policies have a "restoration clause" that allows your benefits to "re-set," even after having used some of them. An example might be when you use some benefits while recovering from hip surgery. After a pre-determined period, such as six months, the full benefit you contracted for is restored.

And here's one more list—some questions you need to ask before signing on the dotted line:

- How much is the daily benefit?
- Will the payments remain "level" (be the same for the duration of the policy)?
- What levels of care does the policy cover and to what extent? Does it cover home health, all levels of nursing home care and custodial care?
- How long must I pay out of my own pocket

(elimination period) before I can start receiving benefits?

- What are the term limits? In other words, what is the dollar limit, the day limit and the year limit?

- Does the policy cover dementia?

- Am I protected against inflation by an inflation rider?

- Can I pay a family member to care for me?

- Will the policy pay for a "private" caregiver (someone who isn't certified and/or licensed)?

A Word of Caution Before Buying
One thing to be aware of is that even big companies that sell long-term care insurance can fail. Penn Treaty had been around for many years and sold insurance policies of many types to many people. In March 2017, the Commonwealth Court of Pennsylvania issued orders placing it in liquidation.

The result of this action was that the State allowed the company to pay out limited benefits to policyholders, leaving many people with less than they paid for. For example, some people who thought they had a lifetime long-term care benefit discovered they weren't going to be covered for life.

When an insurance company is dissolved, the state in which it is registered limits its liability to policyholders according to the state's law. This limitation varies from state to state. It's therefore crucial to do business with an insurance company that is solvent. While there are no guarantees, there is a rating system that can help you. Your best bet is to purchase insurance from a company with one of these ratings: A++, A+, A or A-.

And one more thing. There's a growing trend for insurance

companies to offer "hybrid" policies. An example would be a life insurance product with a long-term care benefit. My opinion is that you should buy the type of policy that you actually need; and that you carefully research whether a hybrid policy is in your best interest.

Using the Benefits
When the time comes to use the benefits, as I said earlier, I suggest you use them sooner rather than later, as this makes life easier for everyone. Many people worry about using them up too soon. Without them, the family *caregiver* is likely to get "used up" too soon.

I also strongly recommend that you get professional help to apply for the benefits. Home healthcare agencies such as mine have people on staff who know how to do this correctly. Making even one mistake can delay the start of benefits by weeks or even months.

7

Caregiver Roulette

The telephone rang one afternoon and the man on the other end of the line said, "My mother is recovering from a broken hip. She's going to need full-time home healthcare for a few months. I want you to send me your best caregiver."

"Send me your best caregiver."

"Thank God you called when you did," I responded. "My best caregiver has been sitting on a shelf for weeks in my office just waiting for your call."

Well, the truth is I said no such thing, but I thought it.

That sort of request is, frankly, ridiculous. The question he should have asked is how do you hire your caregivers? My "best" caregiver is working. So is my second best and likely my third and fourth, too, unless their client passed away yesterday. If they aren't a high quality, credentialed and professional aide, they won't be working for us in the first place.

That can't be said for all agencies, which is why it's important to carefully check out any agency you are considering hiring. Beware of those with a 65-step hiring process—if the person can walk 65 steps from their car to the office, they're hired. That sort of agency is likely to send out the first warm body they can reach regardless of how qualified or appropriate the caregiver is, and you are left watching the "caregiver roulette" wheel spin. The odds of that match-up being a winner are stacked against you.

The important thing is to know who you are doing business with.

Getting back to my story, you need to be aware that there isn't ever one "best" caregiver in an agency, but there is likely to be one "best" caregiver (or two) *for any given client*. Like any relationship, many factors go into making a match, and it's far more than the spin of a wheel. What works for one person doesn't work for another, and what makes it work isn't always obvious. The time and attention a good agency spends on evaluating the relationship dynamics significantly increases your odds of winning at the caregiver roulette game.

Here's one example: Last year a daughter called us to hire a caregiver for her 90-year-old mother who seemed to have given up on life. She and her siblings (who lived out of state) were all delightful and devoted and, I'm sure, thought they were doing the right thing by insisting the caregiver provided be a woman in her fifties—or older. Their logic was that there would be a better chance their mother could relate if they were closer in age.

I didn't agree with their thinking and, instead, sent them a 19-year-old nursing student named "Ashley." My gut feeling, honed by my experience in the field, told me that Ashley, who was loaded with personality and enthusiasm for her job, would be the perfect choice.

They were horrified.

Simply horrified.

At first.

But then, guess what?…Ashley and the client fell in love with each other! Ashley became the "local" granddaughter the

48

woman wanted, and in very short order our client had come out of her shell.

She called me one day to thank me for choosing Ashley for her. She said Ashley had changed her life. Had I let the daughter choose the caregiver, she would have probably chosen someone much older, and the outcome would have been quite different.

And that brings me to the issue of interviewing potential caregivers that come from an agency. "Can I interview the person beforehand?" is one of the most common questions I hear.

What I'm going to say about that will probably surprise you. If you are working with an agency you trust, don't bother interviewing a potential aide. There is *no difference* in the success rate of the client/caregiver choice when the caregiver is interviewed by family members and when she or he is not interviewed by them.

Really? You might be asking.

Yes. Really.

Family members interview from the perspective of their own mindset, not the loved one's mindset. They might choose someone because *they* are comfortable with that person, which is no guarantee their loved one will feel the same way. The candidate might be the best communicator in the world in an interview, but that doesn't necessarily make that person the best caregiver in that situation.

The only way to find out if it's going to work out is to try it and see. Kind of like dating.

There *is* one interview that should be at the top of your list, however, and that is the one you have with potential agencies. The important thing is to know who you are doing business with. Once you have confidence in the agency, butt out and let them do the choosing for you. It is, after all, what they do every single day. They are going to have a far better feel for the right person than you are. (Sorry, I don't want to hurt your feelings, but it happens to be true.)

Here's a little anecdote about a man who asked a home healthcare agency to send someone to his home. After just one day of caring for his wife, who had had elective surgery and couldn't yet fend for herself, he knew caregiving wasn't for him. He was both relieved and nervous about bringing a total stranger into the house, but he was willing to trust the agency and give it a shot. The caregiver turned out to be just what the doctor ordered, and they all lived happily ever after...or something like that.

Not all home healthcare agencies are alike.

Oh, yes. I forgot to mention that that man was me, and I had instructed my agency not to tell me who was coming and not to tell the caregiver who came who I was. It's not uncommon for people who work for my agency not to know me because I'm not in the office much, and I figured it would make her nervous if she knew.

The reason I'm telling you this story is that I want you to know that I know how it feels to be bringing a stranger into the mix when someone you love needs help. But I also want to stress that I did so with the greatest possible confidence not simply because I own the company but because my home healthcare agency conducts business the way it should be conducted to ensure success (and improve the roulette odds).

Just as not all restaurants, attorneys, grocery stores and hair salons are alike, the same goes for home healthcare agencies. You need to do some significant homework before settling on the one you are going to trust with your beloved family member.

You can ask for references if you're so inclined, but HIPAA (privacy) regulations make it unlikely you'll get any. Don't be fooled by fancy websites, glitzy TV commercials or pretty pictures in a brochure. Instead, seek referrals from doctors, hospitals, rehabilitation centers, elder agencies, trusted professionals such as attorneys, and friends.

In preparation, investigate at least three agencies, getting answers to the following questions:

- How long have you been in business?

- Is your agency willing to provide another caregiver if the first one doesn't work out? (Unless you're me, you don't marry the first person you date.)

- Do clients have access to a live person 24/7 if there's a problem or emergency?

- How do you verify your employees' credentials such as citizenship, driver's license and auto insurance?

- Do you conduct a background check?

- What does the agency do if the person cannot make their shift?

- Do you have a competent fallback person?

- Are your caregivers bonded and insured?

- Do your caregivers receive regular training to stay updated? (My agency has an online university. If a caregiver needs more training to deal with a client with a certain condition, they can log on and learn more about it.)

- Do your aides speak understandable English?

- Is the owner involved?

At the end of the day it's a gut feeling about the agency you hire—after you do your due diligence.

I'm a strong believer in choosing franchised agencies rather than independent ones because franchisees have a considerable amount of oversight and can lose their franchise if the business isn't being properly run.

Oh, and here's one more extremely important thing to tell you.

What's more frightening than your ailing parent falling and getting hurt? A caregiver who isn't an employee of a home healthcare agency falling and getting hurt.

I strongly advise against finding your caregiver from a nurse registry (or from an independent source like Craigslist). You might be tempted, because the hourly rate is probably going to be less than the rate from a home healthcare agency, but there are (scary) reasons for that.

Caregivers from nurse registries are most often independent contractors, not employees, and this can put you at financial risk.

Independent contractors are unlikely to be bonded and insured. They are unlikely to be covered under workers' compensation. If they have an accident in your house, you can be sued; and this is not something normal homeowner's insurance covers.

The registry may not be taking taxes out of their paycheck, and if the person doesn't file his or her taxes, the IRS can come to you with bill in hand. That happened to one of our clients, and it took months to resolve.

Also, independent contractors are supposed to be free to set their own schedules and are expected to be experts. Independent contractors get no supervision, no ongoing training and no one to verify that they are keeping up with their skills. In this environment you are the employer, and it's unlikely that you are able to provide that supervision, training and education.

When hiring a caregiver there are some important things to keep in mind.

These are people, not robots or slaves. They may not do everything exactly the way you think they should be done, so choose your battles. You want to build a partnership, not run a dictatorship. If your caregiver doesn't fix chicken the way you would, let it go.

Chill out if she's watching TV or making a phone call while your mother sleeps. This takes nothing away from your parent's safety or comfort.

If you have a problem with the caregiver, discuss it first with the agency, not the caregiver. (By the way, this is not an option if you are using someone from a registry or someone you have hired privately. You have to deal with the caregiver directly in that situation.)

And finally, caregivers are precious resources, people who often do things that you can't, won't or don't know how to do. Never lose sight of that fact and remember to say "please" and "thank you."

Typical duties (ADLs) performed by home healthcare aides (state laws may apply):

Light housekeeping

Laundry

Bed linen changes

Meal preparation

Food shopping

Ambulation and transferring

Bathing and dressing assistance

Taking the client to doctor appointments and other activities outside the home serving as a guide, companion or helper

Toileting

Companionship

Checking pulse, temperature and respiration

Helping with simple, prescribed exercises

Medication reminders

Feeding assistance

Using special equipment such as a Hoyer lift

8

Mom Always Loved You More!

My wife, Irene, and I were enjoying a cocktail and some much-anticipated down time at The Beach Club in Palm Beach one evening around sunset when my cell phone rang. She shot me one of those "Really? You're going to answer it?" looks. "Yes," I reluctantly signaled her, gesturing that I'd make it quick. I'd better—we were overdue for a date night, and if I knew what was good for me, I wouldn't spend my time taking business calls.

"Scott, this is Wendy Matthews," said the pressured voice on the other end. I had spoken to Wendy the day before about care options for her mother Martha who wasn't doing well at home by herself.

"My brother is going to call you in a few minutes," she said without waiting for me to say hello. "Bill thinks I'm nuts, but he's an ass. Don't listen to anything he tells you to do. I know what's best for Mom. He hardly ever sees her. He just flies in from New York three or four times a year and thinks he can just write a check and make everything all better."

"OK, Wendy," I replied. "Could you please ask him to call me tomorrow?"

It was too late. A call was coming in from area code 212 and I was pretty sure that the caller was Bill.

Shoot, I thought to myself (though that probably wasn't the actual word that popped into my head).

"Wendy, I think he's calling me now."

"Remember, Scott, he's not in charge here. I am."

With an apologetic grimace, I took the next call and, sure enough, it was Bill.

"Scott," said the calm, deep voice on the other line. "I understand that you and Wendy spoke yesterday about options for our mother."

"Yes," I replied.

"Well, keep in mind that Wendy is a bit on the neurotic side. She sees monsters in every closet, if you know what I mean."

Uh, OK, I'm thinking to myself.

"I'm in a much better position to make decisions about our mother. Nothing should be entrusted to Wendy or my other sister. Please consult me before anything is done. OK?"

Other sister? I'm still stuck on that new piece of information.

"All right, Bill. I will get back in touch."

"I'm sorry, Irene," I said with that charming smile that still melts her heart (I hope) after 43 years of marriage. Let the date begin.

The phone rang again. Uh-oh.

By now the figurative daggers were starting to feel more like real ones, so I turned off the ringer and put the phone into my coat pocket.

On the way home I listened to my messages.

"Scott, this is Kathy Bellinger," the message began. "I'm Martha Keller's daughter. I understand my sister is looking into care options for my mother. Bill and Wendy have ganged up on me all their lives, and I'm concerned they're going to go behind my back and make decisions about my mother that she won't like. I've been the closest one to her, and she told me a long time ago that if anyone ever had to make life or death decisions for her, it should be me. Please call me right away. Any time tonight is fine, even if it's late."

"He thinks he can just write a check and make everything all better."

Here we go again, I thought to myself. Another dysfunctional family. Another ping-pong match among siblings with their parent being the ball. Another elderly person who was going to suffer for it.

Here we go again...another dysfunctional family.

The sad fact is that there is often incredible disagreement among siblings when their parents start needing help and the old wounds from childhood get in the way. It's something people in my business deal with all the time.

Rebecca might not say she's still angry that her sister Bonnie got a more expensive prom dress than she did, but she is. After all, that meant Mom loved Bonnie more. And so the rivalry continues and even escalates with the magnified stress an aging parent can present. The kids are still, after all these years, vying for a parent's love or financial support.

What's needed at a crisis point in a parent's life is good decision-making, which is severely hampered when brothers and sisters can't agree. Often they're disagreeing more because of the relationship they have with each other than what is in the best interest of their parent.

They likely have no expertise in making the kinds of decisions facing them and are doing so based solely on the fact that they hate each other and want to get back at their sibling(s) to show them who's boss or who loves their parent more. You get the picture.

There is very little difference between these kinds of squabbles and those that divorced parents have over the children caught in the middle. The well-being of a person whose life hangs in the balance often takes a back seat to ego.

A common argument is about whether the parent should stay home. One (usually the brother) wants to write a check, send Mom to a good assisted living community, and go on about his life. His sister, on the other hand, thinks this is cold and unfeeling. "Look at everything Mom sacrificed for you!" A sibling carrying most of the burden of care may get lambasted by a brother or sister for the way that care is being provided and feel unfairly criticized or put upon. One sibling will decide that too much (or too little) is being spent on the parent's care, and a disagreement is born with no good resolution in sight. The number of depressing potential scenarios is endless.

If any of this sounds familiar, do not be surprised. According to the National Alliance for Caregiving, about 20 million Americans are providing care for a parent or in-law. You might be a participant in one of those family boxing matches right now.

So let me ask you a question: Do you see yourself in any of these toxic types of sibling roles?

The Martyr

You stoically trudge along doing what has to be done to take care of Mom or Dad, all the while resenting everyone—and letting them know that you resent them.

The Smart One

You think your way is the best, and you aren't willing to concede that your sibling might be right after all, even now and then.

The Criticizer

You aren't nearly as involved in the care of your parent as your sibling, yet you "Monday morning quarterback" every action and decision your sibling makes.

The "Lawyer"

You argue every single aspect of every single potential option to the point that almost nothing gets done (except arguing).

The Free Spirit

You've spent every dime you ever made, and then some, and are counting on an inheritance to see you through. You don't hang around to do any caregiving, but you don't mind writing yourself a check now and then out of your parent's account.

The Warrior

You have always seen your siblings as adversaries and are primed for battling out every decision until you win.

The Denier

You simply don't believe that your parent is as bad off as your sibling says, and you discount the dire warnings they're giving you.

OK. So now what?

Ahem.....

Time to grow up! OK, so maybe it's not you who's not be-ing the grownup, but that doesn't matter. What does mat-ter is that your parent's care will be determined in large part by how well you can get along with your siblings. While I can't fix old wounds (you'll need to consult your therapist for that) I can at least provide some guidelines that might make this situation a bit easier.

- Make up your mind that you are going to do every thing in your power to work harmoniously with your sibling(s) and ask that they make the same vow. It is, after all, supposed to be about the well-being of someone you all love.

- Hold a family meeting with the goal of assigning tasks to the person best equipped to do them. One person may be better at sorting out the finances while the other is a better researcher who can find out about care options. One may have more time to spend, while the other may have more money. Both are equally valuable.

- Provide regularly scheduled updates about each other's progress on their tasks. This can be done in person, by phone or via e-mail. When everyone is kept in the loop, there's less opportunity for distrust or misunderstanding.

- Discuss from the very beginning what the expec-tations are about finances, and who will be in charge. If this seems like an unsolvable bone of contention, enlist the help of an independent third party such as a family friend to bring reason into the mix. If that doesn't work, you may need to hire an elder mediator or geriatric care manager.

- Designate one child to be the primary caregiver or major decision-maker where care and medical decisions are concerned, and respect the decisions of that person, even if it's a different decision than one you would make. Be supportive in every possible way of your sibling.

- Make sure the primary caregiving sibling has an outlet for respite such as help from a part-time paid caregiver. Caring for an elderly person can put significant stress on the caregiver and negatively affect that person's health and well-being.

- Avoid criticizing the caregiving sibling, especially if you aren't down in the trenches with them and may not be seeing the entire picture.

- Ask the caregiving sibling what you can do to help. Listen, then follow through to the best of your ability.

- If possible, figure out a way the caregiving sibling can be financially compensated.

- If you can't agree on the level of care your parent needs, bring in an expert for a professional opinion, such as a geriatric care manager or even someone like us.

- Make sure that your parent is as bad—or as good— as you believe them to be, before trying to force on everyone else your opinion about what should be done.

- Don't be surprised by gender differences when it comes to points of view. In interviews with 149 pairs of siblings, professor of sociology Sarah

Matthews at Cleveland State University found that sisters expect siblings to be a cooperating team with a lot of communication. Brothers, on the other hand, are likely to act more independently and may negotiate directly with parents without keeping sisters informed.

- Finally, if your parent is mentally competent—or is not yet at a stage where he or she needs any care—hold a meeting with your parent and siblings and ask what your parent would want should the need for help arise. Write it down. Distribute it to everyone and, as much as possible, stick to your parent's wishes when the time comes.

9

My Parents Are Outliving My Money

Alice did not like her son Frank's fiancée one bit, and she had no problem letting Frank know how she felt. Briana wasn't educated enough. She didn't wear her hair right. She was lazy. She would make a terrible mother, and she had the table manners of a baboon at a tea party.

Oh, and one more thing. Alice let Frank know that if he went through with the marriage, Frank would be written out of her will. Any questions?

You can imagine how damaging this manipulative behavior was to their mother-son relationship. Three years later, Alice, who didn't disinherit Frank after all when he married Briana but did boycott the wedding, found out just how bad it was when she had a stroke and Frank became her guardian.

Because of the hostility he felt, Frank brought in the lowest-paid caregiver he could find, and Alice did not get the kind of care she would have wanted or could afford. Why not? Well, that meant more was left for Frank when she died. Payback. Funny how that works.

Using money as a weapon is as old as money itself, and it doesn't matter if it's old money or new money.

Money can be a weapon of family destruction.

Money can be, in fact, a weapon of family destruction. And that's why it's essential you remove yourself from any sort of gamesmanship like that used by Frank's mother; and instead use your time and energy to plan, plan, plan. Way ahead. And let your children know where they stand and what you expect.

Using your money as a weapon against your children will teach them to do the same not only to you but probably with each other as well.

And speaking of children, to expect that those who have warred with each other all their lives will sit down and have a Kumbaya moment, resolving to work cooperatively for your benefit when you are not at your best is, well, just silly. It's not going to happen.

One may want to spend more of the money while the other wants to spend less. One thinks Dad needs a full-time care-giver. The other thinks Dad's just fine with a little help. It gets very complicated and can morph into a very ugly cocktail.

Even without sibling issues muddying the waters, children are known to make really terrible decisions where their parents are concerned for a multitude of reasons. Some are wrapped in the pretty paper of good intentions but filled with bloated ignorance, while others are wrapped in a smelly newspaper of greed like in Frank's situation.

Let's talk for a moment about something parents don't like to think about, or even acknowledge.

Not every child will have their parents' best interests at heart. They may make care (or other spending) decisions based primarily on saving money (more for them later) rather than on what's right for the parent. They may simply be unprepared to make intelligent decisions about their parents' financial or physical well-being, or they might be (to put it indelicately) leeches.

Take the case of Susan, 43. While her brother, Will, became a successful lawyer, Susan hooked up with several "loser guys" and ended up being a single parent with one year of junior college, a part-time clerical job and living in a cottage on her parents' property.

Will suspected for years that his parents were subsidizing Susan and, in his way of looking at it, enabling her dependency, but there wasn't much he could do about it. When their father died eight years ago, however, Will began to feel very protective of his mother and started paying much closer attention to what was going on. He didn't like what he discovered one bit, but he wasn't surprised.

Their mother was writing Susan checks to the tune of about $10,000 a year, in addition to providing her with free rent and paying for most of her food. Will didn't need the money (so that wasn't the issue) but he worried that if his mother kept writing checks to Susan she would run out of money, and then what would happen? Would Susan get off her behind and get a good job and take care of their mother's financial needs? Will doubted it and stepped in. When the checks stopped, Susan became furious at both her mother and brother, threatened to keep her daughter away from her grandmother if her mother didn't "help her out," and the family dissolved into a million glass shards.

Your parents' financial situation is nothing like they expected.

I believe that the very best thing you can do, and do it now, is meet with an elder law attorney. By planning ahead for every conceivable eventuality, there's a better chance your needs will be met the way you would want if you can no longer handle them yourself. Laying out everything ahead of time can also significantly reduce sibling squabbles as well as opportunities for those closest to you to be tempted to make decisions on your behalf that are not in your best interest.

Let's talk now a little about your parents. If they are like millions of the elderly, their financial situation is nothing like they expected for the following reasons:

They have lived longer than they projected.

Interest rates are far lower than they anticipated, so their cash flow is less.

Everything costs more.

Their home equity has plummeted.

Also like a lot of folks from that generation they have saved their money "for a rainy day." It may be up to you to point out that it's raining and raining hard, and they need to get some help quickly.

Does this cut into your inheritance?

Yes. (But not mine. I inherited the "Greenberg" hundreds without incident.)

Should that matter?

I am sure you know the answer to that.

If you're in charge of your parents' money, be positive that you know what you're doing. Make sure you are making spending decisions for the right reasons. Seek expert advice. Don't see your parents' money as your personal cookie jar. I cannot tell you how many people have been deemed ineligible for Medicaid when needing to go into a nursing home because one of their children decided to make themselves a financial gift or two (or three). And in case you're expecting an inheritance, it won't be there if it all goes to a nursing home because Medicaid benefits have been denied since you couldn't wait to get yourself a new car or you used Mom's money to pay for your kids' tuition.

Financial planning of all kinds, including being able to qualify for Medicaid, should be the work of experts. It is not something you should do after reading a few articles on the internet.

Keep in mind that in every family there's the possibility that someone has designs on your (or your parents') money. One out of every five people over the age of 65 will be victimized by some type of fraud, and often that fraud comes from trusted family members.

Money makes people do stupid things...and unkind things... and unethical things.

Don't be a pawn in any sort of those things—wittingly or unwittingly.

Don't let money be a weapon of family destruction in your life.

10

What Happens If You Don't Make It Home Tonight?

My seatbelt was fastened and the seatback tray in front of me was in the upright position as the US Airways jet I was on paused on the taxiway at New York's LaGuardia Airport. It was 8:15 a.m., and we were about to take off for Charlotte, North Carolina where I was speaking at a meeting. Little did I realize that at that exact moment a sinister plan was being executed in Boston which would inflict unimaginable evil and terror on the people of the United States. That day was September 11, 2001, and I have never been the same since.

The words "There but by the grace of God, go I" never meant more to me than it did when I learned upon landing the full horror of what had occurred. It is a sentiment that still rattles the deepest parts of my psyche when I think about that awful day.

I flew all over the country for business in those days and I just as easily could have been flying out of Boston headed for Los Angeles on the ill-fated American Airlines jet.

What would have happened if I hadn't made it home that night?

A few years later after moving to Florida and buying the home healthcare company I now own, I attended a seminar on advance directives and planning given by my friend Michelle Hollister, elder law attorney and Past President of The National Guardianship Association. This is how she began her talk:

"What happens if you don't make it home tonight?"

Chills ran down my spine. There was that question again.

The room got very quiet as I watched the audience creating silent scenarios in their heads of just what that would mean to themselves and those they love.

"How prepared is your family should you suddenly and unexpectedly die?" Michelle challenged. "What if you weren't killed but were severely injured and couldn't speak for yourself? What if you could never live a normal life again? Would you want to be kept on life support? Would your estate go to the people you wanted it to in the way you would like?"

I could see on the attendees' faces that a lot of those questions were ones they not only had never addressed but had probably never even thought about.

So, let me give you the same challenge.

What happens if you don't make it home tonight?

I've discovered that people often believe that a last will and testament is all they need to ensure a smooth and satisfactory transition to those left behind. Nothing could be further from the truth.

A last will and testament is good for a few things including making sure that family heirlooms go to the people you designate and, if you have minor children, designating the person who will care for them if their other parent isn't available.

I'm oversimplifying this, of course, to make a point. But the fact is that it doesn't address anything whatsoever pertaining to your affairs if you live but become incompetent or incapacitated. It is not designed to designate specific people to handle your affairs if you do not die, or to set up legal entities to protect your assets. Expecting a will to take care of every wish and eventuality is kind of like expecting a car with one tire to be equipped to take you on a road trip.

Life won't necessarily unfold the way you expect it to.

I'm not trying to scare you but rather to make you aware that life won't necessarily unfold the way you expect it to.

The good news is that 90% of deaths can be anticipated, which means that only 10% are sudden or unexpected. The problem is that since you have no way of knowing if you'll be part of the 90% or the 10%, you're better off preparing for the latter.

90% of deaths can be anticipated... 10% are sudden.

In this chapter, I'll be outlining the typical documents that well-prepared people make sure to have with the aim of giving themselves and their loved ones peace of mind. Here's my disclaimer: I am not an attorney, and each person's situation is different, so I am not offering legal advice. This information is here for educational purposes only and you must consult an attorney to determine what is right for you.

Speaking of attorneys, do you know the difference between an elder law attorney and an estate planning attorney? People sometimes think they are the same, but they're not, and here's the distinction I find most useful:

Do you know the difference between an elder law attorney and an estate planning attorney?

Elder law attorneys specialize in helping you arrange your affairs and anticipate eventualities that are likely for you during your lifetime. This might include setting up a durable power of attorney or living will (to be defined later in the chapter).

Estate planning attorneys specialize in helping get everything in order that will apply after your death, such as setting up trusts and wills. Again, this is an oversimplification, but I think you get the idea. Notice that I used the word "specialize" where both those types of attorneys are concerned. I encourage you to seek out specialists for these crucial parts of your life and death planning. Just any old attorney won't do. Your son's wife's neighbor's brother might be an excellent personal injury attorney, but he's not likely to be up on the latest laws and regulations pertaining to this type of planning.

Why use an attorney when you can get many, if not all, of the documents you might need through an online legal service? Won't an attorney cost more? Yes, it probably will cost more to use an attorney rather than a website, which can be penny-wise and pound-foolish. The law is complicated, and the laws of each state vary. Do you really want to take a chance that you might overlook something crucial or make a mistake that would end up not having the outcome for your loved ones that you wanted? Personally I'm not willing to take that risk.

Let's talk now about common important documents. Not all documents are needed by all people. It depends on your situation.

Last Will and Testament
Wikipedia defines a last will and testament as "a legal declaration by which a person, the testator, names one or more persons to manage his or her estate and provides for the distribution of his property at death." Anyone with any assets at all, such as a bank account or home, most likely needs a will.

Let me ask you this. If you have a will, when was the last time you looked at it? If it's been more than three years, there's a good chance something has changed in your life that requires a change in your will. Maybe your minor children have come of age or you got divorced or your son ran away to Kurdistan with an exotic girl who doesn't speak English but knows 50 ways to spend his money. Don't lock it away and forget about it. Dust off those cobwebs and take a fresh look.

Living Will

This document specifies whether or not you want to prolong medical treatments in the event that you contract a terminal illness or are in a permanent vegetative state. This directive is not instituted until and unless you are incapacitated and often can only be applied after certification by a doctor or other professional (depending on the laws of your state) that your illness or incapacity is permanent.

DNR

A DNR (Do Not Resuscitate) is a legal order written either by a hospital or other legal entity which states the patient's desire not to undergo any advanced or "heroic" lifesaving measures such as CPR in the event the patient's heart stops or the patient stops breathing. You can't just tell a paramedic or emergency room doctor that the patient has a DNR. Unless you show it to them, lifesaving measures will be taken.

P.O.L.S.T.

This is an acronym for Physician's Orders for Life-Sustaining Treatment. P.O.L.S.T. is not an option in all states and may be called something different in your state (it's called M.O.L.S.T. in New York). The idea behind it is to be more specific about what kind of treatment you want in a situation where you are gravely ill or injured. A DNR order only applies if the heart or breathing has stopped. A P.O.L.S.T., usually prepared by a doctor, can address certain situations such as whether you would want a feeding tube inserted or an infection treated. It is generally of interest to someone with a serious illness or who is very sick. It covers more specifics than a living will, which can be too vague to ensure your wishes.

Power of Attorney

This is a document which allows another person to represent you in legal or financial matters. An example would be someone going to the closing of a real estate purchase and signing for it on your behalf. A regular power of attorney only applies for some particular circumstance or limited time while you are competent. If you die or become incompetent, the power of attorney is negated.

Durable Power of Attorney

This document allows someone to act on your behalf. I have seen unfortunate situations where someone gets dementia and hasn't signed a durable power of attorney, thus tying the hands of their spouse who needs to sell their jointly owned house or cash in jointly owned stocks and cannot do it.

I cannot overstate how important it is for you to know the laws of your state before having such a document executed, however. In the State of Florida, a DPOA becomes effective as soon as it is signed, whether you have been declared incompetent or not. If the person you designate is a nefarious character, the DPOA could be abused even if you're perfectly in control. If that happens, you can kiss your money good-bye.

Trust

A trust allows a third party, called a trustee, to hold onto assets on behalf of beneficiaries. Trusts can be designed many different ways depending on exactly how and when you want your assets to pass to beneficiaries. Because trusts usually avoid probate, assets can pass more quickly to beneficiaries than they might if specified in a will, which can end up in court. It can also help reduce or avoid taxation.

Healthcare Surrogate

This document appoints someone to make medical decisions for you if you are unable to do so. It also allows the doctor to talk to your designated friend or family member about your condition.

People are often surprised to learn that doctors cannot talk to them about their spouse's or their adult child's condition without that person's permission. It gets even more complicated with domestic partners. Without a healthcare surrogate document, you might not even be able to get into the intensive care unit to see your loved one if you are unmarried and are not that person's healthcare surrogate.

"What do you mean you can't talk to me? I'm his wife!"

It is vitally important for you to tell the people closest to you what documents and orders you have and where to find them. Your family needs to know ahead of time what your wishes are so that there is less confusion during a crisis.

Do not keep sole copies of your important papers in a safe deposit box in case they are needed on a Friday night of a holiday weekend and the next time the bank is open is Tuesday morning. If one of those documents is a DNR and you are terminally ill, it won't do you any good in the bank vault. My wife and I each have a flash drive with all our important documents on them that we carry in our wallets.

When delegating who is to take care of what, think about what each interested party does best, and put in writing each person's specific job. One child might be better at making medical decisions while the other would do a better job handling finances.

Craft your paperwork to allow you to be in control for as long as possible. Be careful not to give it up too soon. The irony is that by doing this in advance, it allows you to be in control even though you are no longer in control.

Don't delay in taking care of this. Now is the time when your mind is clear and there's little chance someone is coercing you into something that might not be in your best interest.

Keep in mind that getting these documents done is as much for those you love as it is for yourself. It allows you to be taken care of the way you want and allows your loved ones to just be there with you and for you when their presence is what you need the most. With your wishes documented, the decisions that need to be made are clearer and easier.

I have no idea if I will come home tonight or not, but one thing I do know is that if I don't, everything that could possibly be anticipated and put in writing where my wife and I are concerned has been done. And that's how I show my family that I love them.

11
Smart Phones Make Me Feel Dumb

"Help! I've fallen and I can't get up!" has to be one of the corniest lines ever written for a TV commercial—but it's also one of the most memorable and parodied lines in advertising history. Even though the ad first aired in 1987, people who weren't even born then have incorporated it into their lexicon. Comedians use it to this day to summon a laugh from audiences.

Well, that venerable piece of electronic equipment isn't your grandfather's Life Alert® anymore. No sir-ee. It's still around, but thanks to advances in the technology, if "Mrs. Fletcher" falls now, can't get up and can't push the button, the Life Alert's® fall detection system will make the call for her.

And I think that's a good thing.

But I'm not too sure about some of the other technology redefining our lives. In case you hadn't noticed I'm a pretty opinionated guy, but when it comes to technology I am both in awe of all the amazing inventions already here and coming our way, and scared to death of them, at the same time. Nothing makes me feel dumber than my "smart" phone.

What does technology mean for us? On the plus side, it can help my children know where I am, but I have to ask myself, do I want my children knowing where I am? It can tell my wife how many times I opened the refrigerator today, but do I really want her to start interrogating me about how many snacks I ate when she wasn't looking?

I could put a tracking device on my dentures.

I could put a tracking device on my dentures if I had them and I'd never lose them again but, hey, that would be just plain creepy.

About 25 years ago I read an article in the *New York Times* called "The Electronic Fork" which posed the question: Just because you can make an electronic fork, should you? With that in mind I think we need to carefully evaluate whether the latest bell and whistle device is going to simplify or complicate our life; whether its benefits outweigh the almost certain aggravation and frustration of making it work the way it's supposed to; and whether it was manufactured simply because it was possible to make it. Sometimes the traditional way is just as good or better.

But let me get off my soap box for a minute and talk about the cool stuff.

Let's begin with the electronic fork. Yes. There really is one that vibrates when you eat too fast. It's supposed to keep you from overeating by slowing you down until the food you've shoved in your mouth makes it to your stomach. That's probably not on my bucket list.

A lot of folks keep in touch with their children and grandchildren electronically, which sure beats the old days when you had to wait until the long distance calling rates went down on Saturday afternoon so you could afford to talk longer than the duration of a Life Alert® commercial.

You can get a pill box that sounds a quiet alarm when it's time to take your pill. If you don't take it, the alarm gets progressively louder until you do. If you don't take it after a certain period of time it will send an electronic message to someone you designate who can nag you the old fashioned way.

There are sensors that tell you how many times you got out of bed during the night, apps for how many steps you took during the day and how many calories you ate, and devices you can hook up to your smart phone to help you monitor your blood pressure at any given moment.

Going to the bathroom at night can be safer than ever thanks to sensors that turn on a dim light when you enter the room and a toilet seat that lights up so you don't miss. (I bet my wife would like me to have one of those.) Homes can have shelves installed that come down to you from above or up to you from below at the touch of a button, which can keep you off the floor and not needing "Mrs. Fletcher's" magic button.

You can make a phone call from your wristwatch just like Dick Tracy did back in the days when that was only a figment of a comic book artist's imagination.

There are now "invisible fences" that can be installed around a piece of property that will sound an alarm if someone wanders beyond a pre-established boundary. This can be very helpful if a family member has dementia and is a wanderer.

Technology is changing the delivery of healthcare in ways we can't begin to imagine. With the advent of electronic medical records, all of your providers can be easily connected and see the same information about you. Doctors are already employing robots to do certain surgeries, enabling the procedures to be more precise or go into spaces smaller than they could using the human eye or hand. Hospitals of the future will have doctors caring for patients from faraway locations, monitoring, examining and even doing surgeries from the comfort of their homes. I'm not sure how I feel about that.

Some of these devices let us "age at home" and keep us out of nursing homes longer, and that's certainly a good thing.

What's not so good is that the technology of this brave new world is exploding right at the time when Baby Boomers and their parents are least able to adapt to it. Some of these devices are like jigsaw puzzles on steroids. I gave my grandson an electronic superhero last Hanukkah. I opened up the box with all its parts and closed it back up, hyperventilating. My grandson, who was eight at the time, put it together in five minutes.

We're not completely lost in cyberspace, however. It is estimated that 53% of people over age 65 use the internet, and 70% of those use it daily. The three most common electronic devices used by seniors are the cellphone, computer and music player (iPod or mp3 player).

Despite all the advances in technology there are still plenty of "old-fangled" ways you can make your life better or safer that don't come with an instruction manual the size of the Manhattan phone book.

Take the rubber bathmat, for example. Get rid of mats that have suction cups, because the foot can get caught and you'll fall through the shower door. You can replace it with no slip strips for pennies.

- Turn the water heater down to 120 degrees to eliminate any chance of burns.
- Retrofit the bathroom with a bathtub or shower that doesn't require stepping into.

All-in-all I think technology is a good news story, but not when it comes at the expense of losing the personal touch. My concern is that people have started substituting human touch and physical interaction with the electronic kind— even when they don't have to. It concerns me that family members who live close by are finding it easier to connect electronically. Skyping Grandma is no substitute for stopping by to give her a hug.

Technology has seemingly made us feel more connected. (All of those people wouldn't be emailing you stupid jokes if they didn't think they were your friends, would they?) In reality, I believe we are actually less connected, because we are interacting in person less. We feel plugged in to the outside world, but it's artificial. It's a golden handcuff.

Enjoy the array of marvelous technology that calls to you, but don't allow it to delude you into thinking that's all you or your loved one needs.

And buyer beware. Just because there's a device that does something unique doesn't mean you need it.

Electronic fork, anyone? No thanks. Just pass the potatoes.

Skyping Grandma is no substitute for a hug.

12

Going Out With A Bang: Sex After 60

I walked into a certain senior center (which I won't name) one morning, to encounter the women at the reception desk giggling and snickering like schoolgirls. Of course I was curious about what was so darn funny, so I asked.

It seems that the night before, a group of "mature" singles (60+) had held their monthly get together (with about six women for every man, of course). As one car after the next exited the parking lot, the security guard prepared to lock up the gate. But there was one problem. Two cars remained with no one in sight. After waiting a few minutes for someone to come out of the building, the guard noticed a man sitting behind the wheel of one of the cars. As the guard approached, the man frantically waved him off, signaling to "wait a minute." About five minutes later, the guard saw a woman's head pop up in the passenger side. She then exited the car, got into her own, and they both drove off. It didn't take much deduction to figure out what had happened, and the guard ended up with a good story about that night, but his story wasn't as good as the one the unnamed man had to tell who was sitting in that driver's seat.

Sex, it turns out, is still an important part of life for both men and women well into their later years.

I still chuckle when I think about a story a friend of mine told me with one of those "Oh God, I just bit into a lemon" kind of faces.

One day he went to visit his parents, 85 and 83, who were living in an assisted living community. He knocked on the door several times, but no one answered. Worried, he went down to the office to get a key. He let himself in and heard noises in the bedroom. He looked in and saw his parents naked, red-faced and hysterically laughing. Were they doing it like they had when they were young? Probably not, but that's OK. They were still doing it!

Sex after 60 isn't likely to be the way it was in the good ol' days. Just ask Toby Keith, whose lyrics sum it up for us Baby Boomers: "I ain't as good as I once was but I'm as good once as I ever was."

Without a doubt sex at this age presents its own unique challenges and circumstances. Men have problems with erections, ejaculation and desire. Women can experience vaginal dryness, lowered libido and embarrassment about how they look.

Medical science can help address the medical challenges, and a little knowledge about male psychology can give you ladies a reason to relax if you're worried about your body, so listen up: men don't care if your arms or breasts sag a little or you're not shaped the way you once were. They're not looking at that. They're just happy they're getting lucky. Yes, even at this age.

Thanks to ED drugs (a $5 billion a year business), people over 60 are having more sex than their parents did. And while I'm not going to talk about my sex life I can tell you this: If I had an erection for more than four hours, I wouldn't call my doctor, I'd call a hooker!

Many older people report that sex is better than it was when they were young. It usually takes more time, and this increases intimacy. It's not just about hanging onto your youth (though for some much older ladies it might be about attracting a man who drives at night). No matter how old you are, you need love and affection, and sex is a powerful (and pleasurable) way to get it.

No matter how old you are, you need love and affection.

I've had some fun with this chapter but now I'm going to get serious. Unlike the unfettered and free 60s (1960s, that is), irresponsible sex can be dangerous.

Although sex at this age carries no worries about pregnancy, health risks are very real, exactly the same risks people half your age face.

Case in point: The Villages in Florida, the largest gated over-55 community in the world.

In 2009, the *New York Post* labeled it "ground zero for geriatrics who are seriously getting it on." It described residents having sex in the ubiquitous golf carts and a seedy Viagra black market rivaling some back alleys outside their stately walls. One police officer told the newspaper, "You see two 70-year-olds with canes fighting over a woman and you think, 'Oh, jeez.'" So, you ask, "What's the problem?"

Sexually transmitted diseases.

That's the problem.

STDs have run rampant there.

According to the *Post* article, between 1995 and 2005 STD rates spiraled upward at a breathtaking rate: reported cases of gonorrhea went from 152 to 245; syphilis cases doubled from 17 to 33; and chlamydia jumped from 52 to 115 cases. A local gynecologist told the *Post* reporter that she treated more cases of herpes and human papillomavirus at The Villages than she had when she worked in Miami.

Currently, nearly 50% of all new diagnosed cases of HIV in the United States are predicted to be seniors. People don't realize that 60-year-old men are dating 35-year-old women and, like the educators say, they are sleeping with everyone else that their partner slept with.

That being said, the best thing you can do if you find yourself widowed or divorced and out in the world for the first time in years is to educate yourself about disease prevention. Just like "back in the day" at the local make-out place, a lowly condom could once again be your best friend.

Enjoy!

13

Please Just Make Sure I'm Dead

Years ago there was a delightful TV show hosted by Art Linkletter called *Kids Say the Darndest Things*. You just never knew what bit of wit or wisdom would come out of the mouths of those babes. Well, not long ago I found myself in what I think could have been called Caregivers Say the Darndest Things. This was after a meeting I attended that left me wide-eyed and considering something I had never thought much about before.

As owner of a home healthcare company, I make it a point to be visible in the community among groups who might benefit from what I do. One of those groups is a support group for caregivers of people who have Alzheimer's disease or are survivors of loved ones who had it.

The upbeat topic of this particular caregiver support group was funeral arrangements. No one was knocking down the door for that one, but there were eight brave souls who showed up to talk and learn about what nobody really wants to talk or to learn about.

As we went around the table, each person was asked what they wanted to happen to them when they died. This is what I heard:

- Donate my body to science

- Be cremated and separate my ashes into urns for my two children

- Donate my organs

- Put me in a mausoleum

- Bury me in the ground

- Scatter my ashes from a helicopter

- Bury me alongside my first husband, not my second

- Send my body up North to the family plot

To my amazement every single one of those eight people said something different. Who knew there were so many choices? I sure as heck didn't. I suddenly realized that death isn't all that simple. In fact, it's more complicated than that other inevitability we call taxes.

After I left that day I set out on a mission to find out more and quickly learned that what I had heard at that support group was only a small sampling of possibilities.

I had thought about death, of course. My own father had died a few years earlier, but I hadn't really pondered how many options there were for arrangements and how treacherous the landscape is for family members when no one plans ahead.

I reflected back on my father's funeral and realized that I had spent way too much money on it because (1) he had never expressed his wishes, and (2) I was emotionally off balance and not in a good frame of mind to make a sound financial decision.

Here's my personal cautionary tale.

My father was living in Las Vegas when he died. He had never discussed anything with anybody about his final wishes—at least as far as my sisters and stepmother knew. I flew there from New York, walked into the funeral home and was horrified by what I saw: My father was "resting" in a plain pine box. Now, this happens to be Jewish custom, so I shouldn't have been all that shocked, but I was. After all, he was my father, and I was in a position to see that his send-off was far fancier than that. So, guess what I did?

I forked over $5,000 for an extravagant casket for him. Well, in hindsight it wasn't really for him.

It was more for me. I wanted to feel better about it, to do one last generous act for him. I wasn't thinking clearly. It might not even have been what my father would have wanted.

It might not even have been what my father would have wanted.

When there are no plans in place, families really don't have a sense of what their loved one wanted. When you make decisions at the time of crisis, you will almost always overspend.

Also, when siblings don't know their parents' wishes this can cause conflict. "Dad would not have wanted it that way," one will say, while the other insists, "That's exactly what Dad would have wanted." It can get even more complicated when there are half brothers and sisters and stepparents involved.

Death should be a time to grieve and remember, not to make complicated decisions. You leave a mess behind if there are no instructions about what you want done.

Death should be a time to grieve, not make complicated decisions.

In most cases, this is simply inexcusable. Only about 10% of deaths are sudden and unexpected. That means 90% of us will have the time and opportunity to do this one tremendous act of love for our families.

Because there are so many questions that come up these days, the best thing your parents can do for you, and the best thing you can do for your children, is to get this out in the open, make the hard decisions, let everybody know about them, and go on enjoying your life.

Virtually every issue within a family pertaining to a death occurs because nobody planned for it.

Get a grip on the financial, emotional and familial implications of your death to avoid family squabbles, confusion, misunderstanding and unnecessary expense.

Here are some examples of the types of questions that should be answered by you for your children and by your parents for you:

Do you want to be buried or cremated?

If you want to be cremated, what should be done with your ashes? Who should get them? Should they be kept or spread? If spread, where, how and when?

If you want to be buried, should it be under a shady tree, next to Grandma or above ground in a mausoleum?

If you choose a mausoleum, which one? On which floor?

Is there already a purchased plot? If so, where is it? If not, where would you like to be buried? This is particularly important to establish for people who have homes in two different states.

If you've bought a cemetery plot or pre-need contract and you move, how does that affect your benefits? Can you get a refund? If so, how and how much?

Do you want to be buried alongside your spouse? If so, should it be side-by-side or head-to-toe?

What if you want to be buried and your wife wants to be cremated? Does she want her ashes with you in your casket or somewhere else?

What if you and your spouse practice different religions? For example, if you want to be buried in a Jewish cemetery, can your non-Jewish wife be buried there, too?

If you were married before, do you want to be buried with your previous or your most recent spouse?

"Bury me next to my first husband, not my second."

If you're a veteran, do you want to be buried in a veteran's cemetery? Which one? Is that OK with your spouse?

Do you want your arrangements to follow your religious background to the letter or is there room for deviation? For example, cremation has been a big no-no among Jews for centuries, but many Jews these days are choosing it as a more economical option.

Who do you want in charge of your final arrangements? You should designate someone, along with an alternate.

Do you want a headstone? If so, what kind? What size? What do you want it to say? (I joke with my golfing buddies that my headstone should say, "This is Scott's first hole-in-one," since I've never had one—at least not yet.)

Do you want a funeral or a memorial service or nothing at all? If you want a service, where should it be?

You get the point...for something so complex it amazes me that most of us are pretty much clueless.

Now, as long as we're on this very maudlin subject, I want to give you another list. This one involves documents that will be needed after you die (or in at least one case, beforehand).

You not only need to have these documents, but you also must, and I repeat *must*, let key family members know that you have them and where they are. You can give them to your attorney or have them in a secure place at home that trusted family members know how to access. The kindest thing you can do is have every pertinent document in one place so that it's not a hardship on your family to try to collect them.

Please note that I am not an attorney and this is not intended as a complete list, but it represents many of the most commonly-needed documents:

- Original copy of your will.

- Ownership documents of all valuable assets such as real estate, cars, cemetery plots, investments and business partnerships.

- A list of all your bank accounts with online login information.

- Tax returns from the last three years (obviously you will need to update these over the years).

- Copies of all life insurance policies. While an insurance company is bound to pay agreed-upon death benefits when a claim is submitted, they are not required to keep track of whether you are still alive. If your family doesn't know about these policies, they won't be able to collect on them.

- Copies of all accounts containing pensions, IRAs, stocks and bonds.

- Location of all safe deposit boxes, along with the keys. Make sure one of your family members is on the registration document so they can access the boxes.

- Healthcare Power of Attorney, so healthcare decisions can be made if you are unable to do so.

- Marriage certificate, so your spouse can prove that you and he/she were married.

- Copy of child support orders.

Consult an attorney to determine all of the documents that your particular situation calls for.

NOTE: *Think carefully about any documents you might be considering keeping in a safe deposit box, as most boxes cannot be accessed 24/7.*

The takeaway of this chapter is that it's really important to let your family know what your plans are; make those plans in advance; understand what you are buying; insure that your wishes are honored; and to give your family the gift of allowing them to grieve.

Oh, and one more thing. You can learn a lot about pre-need planning on the internet. One good website is www.dignitymemorial.com.

Now, go out and eat a good meal.

Tell someone special you love them and enjoy the rest of your life.

14

You're Never Too Old To Have A Purpose

The purpose of life is not to be happy. It is to be useful, to be honorable, to be compassionate, to have it make some difference that you have lived and lived well. — Ralph Waldo Emerson

In 2007, I went to the funeral in New York of a dear friend who had died at 62 of pancreatic cancer. She was a wonderful wife and mother, a successful realtor in New York and Florida, and was a champion amateur golfer. The room was packed. People had flown in from all over the country. I said to a friend sitting next to me, "Damn, would you look at this crowd!" I knew she was well-known, but this was over the top. My friend replied to me, "When you're the first to go, everybody shows up. When you're the last, your service is at the graveside, and they just roll you in."

It was kind of funny, but it also rang true, and it got me thinking about people who have reached the age where many of their friends are gone, often their spouses are gone, and their lives look absolutely nothing like they did 5 or 10 years earlier.

I see it in my business all the time—clients who've become progressively more isolated and, as a result, are depressed, feeling hopeless and just waiting for their turn to get rolled into the grave. They've stopped playing cards three times a week. They no longer go out to dinner with friends, and the widows' club they were active in has shrunk from eight to three, one with dementia and the other two unable to drive. Before you know it they are spending more and more time alone in front of the TV doing crossword puzzles and never leaving the house.

Nobody depends on them, and they don't depend on anyone.

How many times have you heard stories about people who were dead for days because there was no one checking on them, and no one knew anything was wrong?

It really bothers me when I hear about people in any of those circumstances because I know that, in almost every situation, incorporating one small change could make all the difference in how they feel about their lives and the time they have left.

That small change is monumentally important: It is to find a purpose, a reason to get up in the morning.

Finding a purpose can happen at any age, and it can take different forms throughout our lives. Raising your children might have been a purpose 40 years ago. Working side-by-side with your spouse to build a future for your family could have filled that place. Taking care of an ill parent might have been your purpose a few years later. And now? You are left thinking you're too old and there's no way you can contribute to the world.

Stop! Do not pass Go! Do not collect $200!

You can sit back and bemoan your situation (Waah! Waah! Nothing is like it used to be!) and get progressively more depressed, passive and resentful like the woman in this Yiddish joke whose son finally calls. Here's their conversation:

Son: "Mom, you don't sound so good."
Mom: "I haven't eaten in four days."
Son: "Why?"
Mom: "I didn't want to be in the kitchen in case you should call."

Your other choice? Take control, get off your behind and find something to do where your talents, skills and wisdom can be applied and appreciated. Once I retire, I want to stay so busy with life passions that my children need a GPS device to keep track of me.

One of the best ways you can find a purpose is to volunteer (this is a far different experience than writing a check, which you should also consider doing, if you can afford to).

It doesn't matter if you can't drive or you have physical impairments or your typing is rusty or your wardrobe isn't fashionable. There is *something* you can contribute to society, and trust me when I tell you, you will get far more out of it than the people will who you help.

Let me tell you a story about myself. I grew up very poor in a low-income neighborhood in Queens, New York, and was an underperforming student in school. Because of my lousy grades and no family connections to grease the skids, there wasn't a single college I applied to that would accept me. Even open enrollment schools rejected my applications. To give myself something to do while I figured out my path in life, I began volunteering with an organization that helped developmentally challenged children. I loved it, and the man

You never know where volunteering will lead.

who ran the organization was so impressed with me that he wrote a recommendation letter for me which resulted in my finally being accepted into college.

Another big plus, one I could never have imagined, was that a pretty young woman named Irene was also volunteering for that organization, and that's how I met my wife of 47 years!

The point of this is that you simply never know where volunteering will lead. There is something magical about giving back and volunteering, and that magic has the potential to change a life (yours as well as others').

I knew a man whose son died tragically in his 30s. The father went into a deep depression and stayed there for years. Nothing seemed to help. Eventually he began mentoring a young boy, and slowly his depression subsided. That boy, now a young man, loves to tell how my friend changed his life. My friend always responds, "Yes, but you changed my life even more."

Volunteering is good for your mind and body. People who volunteer tend to be healthier and happier because they have a purpose. Volunteering forces you to get up and take a shower and put on clean clothes and get out of the house. If you're having a bad day, you still have a reason to get up. You meet new people, make new friends and now have folks in your life who would check on you if you didn't show up when you were supposed to.

Engaging yourself in something meaningful and challenging helps keep your mind young. Socializing reduces isolation.

Ask yourself what kinds of causes and issues interest you. Disadvantaged or sick children? Handicapped people? Animals? Diseases like breast cancer? Battered women? Education?

The list is endless.

Now here's the tough love part: No one is going to beat down your door to volunteer. You have to be proactive by picking up the phone and making some calls; or contacting friends and family to find out what they are doing that you might enjoy. The following list will give you an idea of where to start. You can get more ideas, and more information about volunteering, at www.worldvolunteerweb.com.

Churches
Synagogues
United Way
Senior centers
Public and private schools
Food banks
Soup kitchens
Veterans' organizations
Mentoring programs like Foster Grandparents
   and Big Brothers/Big Sisters

Volunteering impacts the community, gives you motivation for life, offers the opportunity for you to achieve something, allows you to utilize your abilities and talents, and introduces you to new people. Once you start, there will always be someone whose eyes light up when you walk into the room. It's unbelievably powerful...I think you get the picture.

It's never too late to experience those benefits. It's in everyone's best interest when a senior shows up and does something good for someone else. If you're housebound, there are organizations you can assist from home, doing phone work or licking envelopes.

The only thing that is holding you back from changing your life for the better is you. I've volunteered all my life, and I've never regretted one day of it. Do something about it today. The quality of your life and your mental health depend on it.

15

Don't Be A "Fallen Woman (Or Man)"

I don't trip. I do random gravity checks.
I did not fall. The floor looked sad so I thought it needed a hug.
Our phones fall, we panic. Our friends fall, we laugh.
Sex on the television can't hurt you—unless you fall off.

In popular culture, falls are humorous. Starting in the late 1920s, it was The Three Stooges who sent people rolling in the aisles with their pratfalls.

In popular culture, falls are humorous.

Actor Dick Van Dyke's fall over the ottoman into his fictional living room was aired every week in the opening footage of *The Dick Van Dyke Show* in the early 1960s, accompanied by canned laughter.

Beginning in 1975, actor and comedian Chevy Chase made a career out of funny tumbles, skids and lurches on *Saturday Night Live*. These became known as the show's "Fall of the Week." He frequently satirized the missteps of then-President Gerald Ford, who had so many unfortunate clumsy moments he was dubbed the "First Klutz." (President Ford reportedly took the ribbing good naturedly.)

Even I (not a renowned comedian) have elicited some laughs (and one scowl) by falling.

One day I was on the golf course and fell when I stepped into a gopher hole. I went down like a tree, and my friends thought it was hilarious.

On another day, a stormy one, I exited Publix carrying an umbrella in my left hand and a bag of groceries in my right. I tripped and fell into the middle of an open parking space. Unlike my friends on the golf course, the person who wanted that open space was *not* amused. He gave me a dirty look (I suppose because I was blocking where he wanted to park) and kept going. That was an example of someone not taking a fall seriously (or having bad manners).

Fortunately, both times only my pride was hurt.

Unfortunately, that's not always the case, especially when it comes to older people.

Approximately, 50% of all ER visits by seniors are the result of a fall, and falls are responsible for 55% of injury deaths among seniors (followed by motor vehicle traffic accidents, suffocation, poisoning and fire). If you're over 80 and fall and break a hip, you're unlikely to ever see the inside of your house again.

If you're over 80 and fall and break a hip, you're unlikely to ever see the inside of your house again.

That's what happened to my mother-in-law, Dinah, whom you read about in Chapter Two. She fell while waiting for a bus, broke her hip, needed surgery and died two weeks later.

It's important to think about the potential devastation of a fall *before* it occurs and take measures to minimize those risks.

My agency frequently receives calls from panicked, out-of-town children whose parent has fallen and now needs help in the home. Think how much better the situation would have been if the fall had been prevented in the first place. Instead of making emergency plane reservations to come see Mom in the hospital, they could be making vacation plans to come visit her at home.

While falls can occur anywhere, they most often occur at home. And that's actually good news. Why? Because many falls in the home are preventable. You just need to be aware of fall risks and dangers around the house and proactively reduce those risks.

While falls can occur anywhere, they most often occur at home.

First, let's talk about what you can do to fall-proof the home. Here's a partial list:

- Remove throw rugs and replace shag carpeting. Both can catch on shoes and walkers.

- Put nightlights everywhere in the house, particularly in the bedroom and bathroom and/or install motion sensor switches on the lights in every room.

- Keep the floors clutter-free, especially the path between the bedroom and bathroom.

- Remove old suction cup-type bathmats. As the suction cups deteriorate, the corners can turn up and catch the foot. Replace with non-slip strips.

- Take frequently-used items out of high places and put them where they are easily-accessible; or install shelves that can be pulled down.

- Get a grasping tool for retrieving objects high up or down low.

- Mount a handheld shower head and a bench in the shower or get an inexpensive transfer bench that will fit across the side of the tub for sliding over into the tub.

- Install a raised toilet seat.

- Put a grab bar in the shower/tub area. It's not too pretty but it's better than grabbing the towel bar, which isn't designed to hold a person's weight.

- Install good lighting in stairwells.

- Remove all unnecessary furniture and all furniture that isn't stable.

- Position furniture in such a way that the person can go from one room to the other as they move safely about the house.

- Remove all electrical cords in walking areas. If necessary, relocate lamps and appliances to keep the cords in a safe location.

Other common risks that need to be evaluated are *shoes, medication, health* and *lifestyle*.

Shoes
Dangerous shoes increase the risk of falling. These include loose, worn or backless slippers with smooth soles, slip-on shoes like flip-flops and sling backs, shoes with slippery or worn soles and shoes with heels higher than one inch and/or a narrow heel.

Good, safer shoes have a slip-resistant sole, a high back around the ankle, laces or Velcro fasteners, heels under one inch and a wide opening to get the foot in and out more easily.

Medication
Sedatives, sleeping pills, anti-depressants, anti-psychotic drugs and the combination of several medications along with over-the-counter vitamins and supplements can all increase the risk of falls. Ask your pharmacist to review all medicines and over-the-counter products your loved one is taking. The pharmacist is a doctor of pharmacy and is the most credible

professional to advise you on drug interactions that may be increasing the chances of a fall.

Health

Staying physically active is an excellent way to reduce your chances of falling and minimize the damage a fall might do to the body.

Regular exercise improves muscles and makes you stronger

It also helps keep your joints, tendons and ligaments flexible. Mild weight-bearing activities, such as walking or climbing stairs, may slow bone loss from osteoporosis.

Have eye and hearing tests

Even small changes in sight and hearing may cause you to fall. When you get new eyeglasses or contact lenses, take time to get used to them. Always wear your glasses or contacts when you need them. If you have a hearing aid, be sure it fits well and wear it.

Core strengthening is good as well

Here's an example of a core-strengthening exercise from Pamela Ellegan on healthyliving.azcentral.com:

The Bridge

The Bridge utilizes isometric contraction to develop strength in your buttocks, lower back and abdominals and improve balance. Begin by lying on your back with your knees bent and feet flat on the floor. Breathe steadily while you contract your core and raise your hips until they form a straight line between your knees and your chest. Do not arch your back. Hold for a count of three before returning to the starting position. Repeat five times.

Lifestyle

Many older people begin to fear falling as they age, which can lead to their avoiding activities such as walking, shopping, gardening and taking part in social activities. Avoiding life can result in further physical decline, depression, social isolation and feelings of helplessness.

Encourage your loved one to reconnect socially

This reconnection can lead to being more active, which can help maintain or improve physical health and may ultimately prevent falling.

Limit alcohol consumption

Studies show that the rate of hip fractures in older adults increases with alcohol use.

Even a small amount of alcohol can affect one's balance and reflexes. Studies show that the rate of hip fractures in older adults increases with alcohol use.

Get enough sleep

Being drowsy is a recipe for falling.

Stand up slowly

Getting up too quickly can cause your blood pressure to drop, making you feel wobbly. Put both hands on the arm of the chair when rising.

Be cautious when walking on wet or icy surfaces

Use an assistive device like a cane or walker when necessary (don't let pride or stubbornness get in the way). Make sure the device is the right size and, if it has wheels, rolls easily.

Get a fall detection device

It can be worn around around your neck or wrist. This is different from a device that has a push button. If you fall the wrong way you might not be able to push the button. A fall detection device issues an alert if it senses a fall.

To summarize: A fall impacts everyone in the family. Be proactive rather than waiting for a crisis. Don't wait for something to happen. Don't wait to help ensure that your loved one is safe and protected. Even small changes can prevent a tragedy.

If you get pushback from your loved one, you may need to be brutally frank: If they break a hip, they might never go back home. You can't let them put themselves in danger without fighting the good fight. Don't be complicit in their fall. You aren't taking control away from them but are working together to remove obstacles that could prevent them from living independently.

Safety is something even warring siblings can usually agree on. It's low-cost and, frankly, I consider it a no-brainer.

A fall impacts everyone in the family. Be pro-active rather than waiting for a crisis.

16

Living With Chronic Disease

It's one of those good news-bad news scenarios: life expectancy in the United States is almost 20 years longer than it was in 1935 (79.3 years vs. 59.9 years).

The good news is obvious, but the bad news is that more and more people are spending those extra years of life dealing with chronic illness, thanks to improvements in medical care that keep people alive longer.

One of my early careers was selling insurance. I used to suggest to my clients that they buy a disability policy that would cover them for no more than two years because, I'd say, you'll either be better by then or be dead. I wasn't being flippant. It's just that in those days if you got a serious illness, you didn't usually survive too long.

Today it's a very different story. Not only are more and more people living with chronic disease, but as a natural extension of that situation, more and more people are being tasked with caring for someone with a chronic disease. There have been entire industries born out of this new normal, ranging from home care services like mine to universal design (an architectural concept that combines esthetics with functionality inside the home).

Chronic disease takes a toll on everybody in the family, especially the spouse or another family member dealing with the day to day caregiving responsibilities. It can be all-consuming and devastating to the caregiver by creating unrelenting stress. With some chronic diseases you could end up taking care of that person for 12-15 years or longer!

This chapter takes a look at several of the major aspects of dealing with chronic disease, illuminating the path that has been shown to ease the burden somewhat for the caregiver. There's also a moving true story at the end of this chapter about one woman's courageous journey of love as she tirelessly cared for her husband who lived two and a half years after being diagnosed with ALS.

Making the most of life
After the initial shock of the diagnosis, creating a healthy mindset should be your first order of business.

Those who weather this situation best resolve early-on to make the most of the years their loved one has left.

Think of your loved one (or yourself) not as *dying* of a chronic disease but as *living with* a chronic disease.

The person is still alive. They still have a life, and there are things that can continue to give that person's life meaning. Find joy in the journey. Resolve to make the very best of the remaining years. Framing how you look at the situation can significantly impact the quality of the life ahead.

Even in the case of dementia or Alzheimer's disease, focus not on what is lost but what has been preserved. There's always something of who that person once was that remains intact. Perhaps they can't remember everything, but they can probably remember some things (in long-term memory).

Maybe they've lost their ability to play golf, but they can still enjoy an indoor putting green.

We must change the perception of chronic disease from being a death sentence to being a life sentence of opportunity—an opportunity to examine our lives.

The stages of grief after diagnosis

Although the diagnosis of a chronic disease isn't an actual death, it is in fact, death of life as you knew it. You can expect to go through most of these stages:

Guilt/shame: Here are some typical examples. Maybe I didn't feed my husband well enough, maybe we didn't go to the doctor when we should have...(there are dozens of things to make you second-guess yourself). Maybe your loved one can't remember names anymore or has deteriorated physically and feels unattractive and is embarrassed. Maybe you're a very private person and aren't comfortable portraying anything but perfection in your private life.

Denial: You think that the diagnosis might have been wrong, that your loved one feels "just fine" and therefore *is* fine, or s/he is "going to beat this thing," despite all signs to the contrary.

Bargaining: There might be pleading..."If this goes away, I promise to be a better person."

Anger: You may go through the "why me?" stage, or be angry at yourself, your spouse or someone else (or God) for not doing something differently.

Sadness: You may go into a depression. Some people can "snap out of it," while others may need medical or psychological help.

Acceptance: This is the stage where you feel more at peace with the situation. You stop fighting it and decide to work with what you have and keep moving forward. This is the stage where living can begin again.

It takes a village

You're no good to your loved one if you have bent so far under the pressure that you break.

Caring for someone with a chronic illness can take a terrible toll on the caregiver. You may have married "for better or worse," but seek out as much help as you can find. You're no good to your loved one if you have bent so far under the pressure that you break. If you aren't around to do the caregiving, what happens to your loved one?

Research shows that 64% of family caregivers of people with Alzheimer's disease who don't get help will pre-decease their loved one!

I'm a big fan of support groups. Chronic disease is isolating for both the patient and the caregiver, and I consider these groups to be critical. Support groups are a great way to meet others going through a similar situation. It's where you'll feel understood as well as pick up some practical coping tools and tips.

Here's an example:
My company sponsors an Alzheimer's disease support group. At a recent meeting, one member told the group how she was struggling at dinnertime to get her husband to eat, even though she prepared his favorite dinner foods. When she remarked that she never had trouble getting him to eat breakfast, another member suggested she give him breakfast food at dinnertime. She tried it and, guess what? He ate it with no problem whatsoever—thanks to a simple idea from a support group that made her life easier.

Going to a support group gives you a little respite from your caring duties. It also allows you to cry in a safe environment and to realize you are not alone.

Many groups will have a place where you can safely leave your loved one. If not, arrange for a friend or neighbor to be home while you are out. It's worth it.

Keep in mind that a support group is likely to grow even more important as you see the social life you once enjoyed shrink and disappear.

Don't isolate yourself
Chronic disease is an isolating process. The key is to get other people involved, because little by little the life you knew is slowly going away.

It can start with something small, like no longer going out to dinner once your loved one can't read a menu or easily get in and out of the car.

Perhaps you were part of a couples group that now excludes you. A lot of times people are uncomfortable with your new normal and start avoiding you. In some cases, believe it or not, people avoid you because they think the chronic disease is contagious.

Your children and grandchildren may also stop visiting as frequently. They may feel uncomfortable and not know what to say or do.

Don't allow that to happen without speaking up. Let people know you need them. It's better to share a burden than to try to handle everything yourself.

Let people know you need them. It's better to share a burden than to try to handle everything yourself.

Instead of getting angry about people distancing themselves, give them tools to do something meaningful. That sort of planning ahead can be a game changer.

Come up with activities family members can share with your loved one. Have your grandchild download some music from that person's era on their iPad and play it for them; or get out photo albums and look at old pictures. In the case of my father-in-law, who had been a cartographer, we could have collected some maps and looked at them together.

Did your loved one used to play cards? Have a card game, real or pretend. Go to the beach. Take a walk. Splurge on an ice cream cone.

Listening to those who care

You'll undoubtedly have well-meaning friends and family pressuring you to try some "magic" solution or cure. Some will say do (or don't) place your loved one in a care facility. Don't dismiss them out of hand but instead carefully consider if these suggestions have merit or not.

It's always a good idea to bounce ideas off of a neutral third party. That's where a support group adds value, as does someone like your doctor, your clergy or a concerned friend.

Finding outside help

Don't expect to get much help from Medicare. You'll be surprised at how little they provide for people with a chronic illness. Medicare doesn't typically cover costs of home care, nor does it cover assisted living or memory care living. Medicare is a restorative program designed to get the patient better. It's not a maintenance program.

Don't expect to get much help from Medicare.

Medicaid is a different story. It can be a maintenance program and isn't just for the poor. Consult a certified Medicaid planner to learn what options you may have in your particular state.

Pick up the phone and call the association dedicated to your loved one's chronic disease. These folks can turn you on to local resources, including any types of programs that might provide funding for caregivers, equipment or other type of assistance. You will find website addresses for a few of the major organizations at the end of this chapter.

Don't overlook local adult daycare centers and faith-based organizations like Catholic Charities and the Jewish Community Center.

Was your spouse in the military? The VA will often provide help you can't get anywhere else.

Find the highest-qualified, preferably board certified, medical professional in your area to treat your loved one. Make sure he or she is a specialist who is up on the latest developments.

Seek out and take part in a clinical trial. Don't worry about being a "guinea pig." Keep in mind that the first person to be cured of any disease is someone in a clinical trial. If your loved one gets the placebo in the trial, they will eventually get the actual drug if the researchers discover that it works. There are 100 reasons not to be in a clinical trial but one really good reason to do it that trumps all the others—your loved one might be the one who is cured.

Seek out and take part in a clinical trial.

Make your wishes known

Make sure your children and all impacted family members understand the wishes of the person with a chronic disease. If you don't want to be kept artificially alive, let everyone know that. Let them know what you want done after you die. This is an important action even if you haven't been diagnosed with a chronic disease because it can take some of the emotions out of it at the time of your death. (See Chapter 10— What Happens If You Don't Make It Home Tonight?)

Useful Resources

American Heart Association
http://www.heart.org

American Cancer Society
https://www.cancer.org/

Alzheimer's Association
http://www.alz.org/

National Parkinson Foundation
http://www.parkinson.org/

ALS Association
http://www.alsa.org/

Multiple Sclerosis Foundation
https://msfocus.org/

One woman's story of courage, determination and unconditional love

Rebecca and her mother, Vanessa, were sitting in front of a computer intently researching vacation options in Puerto Rico. Vanessa and her husband, William, had talked for years about going, and it was finally time.

The couple, who had met in college, had done a lot of traveling in their 44 years together, but there was now a sense of urgency they'd never felt before.

Just the day before, the family had gotten awful news— William had ALS, also known as Lou Gehrig's disease. He wouldn't be getting better. Every day he was likely to get just a little bit worse until he couldn't move, speak, swallow or breathe on his own. The road ahead promised to be tough for everyone.

William had been deteriorating for a year before the diagnosis. He was already using a walker and a wheelchair to get around, but that didn't keep them from making this trip. Within five weeks Vanessa and William were on a plane, sipping rum in Puerto Rico, holding hands and delighting in the country's beautiful beaches and island culture. It was their last out-of-town trip together and the beginning of a two and a half year journey marked by stolen solitary tears, frustration, research, phone calls and a surprising amount of joy.

Looking for the joy in everyday life
"When William was first diagnosed, I cried a lot but never let him see it," said Vanessa. "We decided from the first moment we heard the news that we were going to enjoy as much of every day as we could."

Vanessa and William made a point to leave the house every day until it became too difficult and precarious for William to get into the family car. Sometimes they went for a meal and drinks at a seaside restaurant. Other times Vanessa would park by the ocean and wheel William along the sidewalk where both took in the warm sea breeze and watched the pelicans swoop down to dive for their dinner. Some days they just took a drive up the coast from their home in Ormond Beach, Florida. When William could no longer easily leave the house, they signed up for Netflix and passed their evenings watching TV series and movies.

Even in the midst of tragedy, their conversations were frequently fun. William hadn't lost his wicked sense of humor. His entire life he had enjoyed national politics. His witty, satirical or sometimes just corny comments about politicians made people both wince and laugh. William didn't let up on this lifelong habit for two and a half years, until the last two weeks of his life when talking became too difficult.

Some of the conversations weren't fun, though, like the one they had about moving to Oregon, where assisted suicide is legal. That option quickly fell by the wayside because by the time William had received his diagnosis, his condition was deteriorating too rapidly for a cross-country move.

The crusade to find help

After returning from their last vacation together, Vanessa went into high gear. Besides interacting with William's doctors, she investigated options from Medicare, the ALS Foundation and the VA. William had served in the U.S. Army and had been in Vietnam during the conflict. The couple suspected that his exposure to the herbicide Agent Orange had been a major factor in his developing ALS, although the U.S. Army has never acknowledged such an association.

Vanessa quickly discovered that Medicare had little to offer. The ALS Foundation loaned them a lift chair, but the VA had one William liked better. It turned out that they got the most help from the VA, including some paid in-home help and medical equipment.

They were just grateful they had enough savings to pay for things that no other agency or organization would pay for such as an electric scooter William used before needing a wheelchair.

Life changes

Vanessa did her best to keep life feeling normal, but there was nothing normal about it. When it got to be too much, she would walk to a nearby park or sit by the water. Sometimes she meditated. Other times she released with tears.

She moved William's bed downstairs and slept by his side every night on a pull-out couch. She didn't sleep much, though. Her ear was constantly tuned to the sound of the

BiPAP machine that kept William breathing, and she worried constantly about the possibility William might choke. "I barely slept for two and a half years," Vanessa said.

Each night Vanessa made William's favorite foods. As his disease progressed she had to puree them.

One day, while William could still speak well, he had Vanessa record him on video during which he told her and Rebecca how much he loved them and how they had both given him such a happy life.

Social isolation and family support

Even before William's diagnosis, Vanessa's social isolation had begun. Once he had started showing signs of *something* (not being able to walk across the room without leaning on the furniture, and being unable to go up the stairs without stopping multiple times) Vanessa simply didn't have time to do anything but take care of her husband.

"I had nurses, physical therapists, occupational therapists and others coming to the house all the time," Vanessa recalled. "My big outing? Going to the grocery store! I got excited on those days because it meant getting out of the house and doing something."

Fortunately she and the couple's only child, Rebecca, were extraordinarily close emotionally and geographically (they are next door neighbors), so Vanessa had some occasional relief, and daily social interaction with Rebecca and Rebecca's husband.

Never losing his awareness, William insisted that Vanessa and Rebecca go out to lunch every Monday while a caregiver, who came for a few hours every day, stayed with him. That help was necessary because in the last year of William's life,

Vanessa was unable to get William in or out of bed by herself, despite having a lift.

The end of life
Fortunately, William never had to suffer the most cruel, end-stage phase of ALS. Two and a half years after his diagnosis, when he could no longer do anything for himself but was still extremely alert, he experienced congestive heart failure and spent 11 days in intensive care. During his hospital stay he contracted MRSA and cellulitis and passed away quietly one night with Vanessa, Rebecca and several extended family members by his side.

"It was a blessing that he didn't have to go through the last stages of ALS," said Vanessa. "His body was so tired he just couldn't fight it."

Picking up the pieces and finding joy again
It took Vanessa more than a year to pick up the pieces of her life and to be able to speak of William without crying, but today she remembers him with a smile, love and a mountain of admiration.

"He never felt sorry for himself and never complained about his situation," she said. "He appreciated the life we had together and what we did for him when he got sick. I'm just glad I was young and healthy enough to take care of him at home. We had a great love story right to the end. And always said I love you each day."

17

Social History

Irene and I were headed to work one morning in 1971 when our car broke down on Metropolitan Avenue in Queens. (This was way before the advent of the cell phone.)

We were a little unnerved—but not much—because we had two things going for us: Irene's father, Lenny, took that same road every day to his job as a fabric salesman in the men's garment industry; and Lenny applied a rigid schedule to every aspect of his life (yes, he was probably a bit OCD).

Glancing at my watch I remarked to Irene, "Don't worry. Your father should be passing here in about eight, no seven, minutes. I'll stand out by the road and flag him down." And guess what...that's exactly what happened.

Fast forward 28 years. Lenny was 80 years old and living in a nursing home. Dementia had robbed him of much of the essence of the energetic, accomplished man he had once been. Caregivers eventually had to feed, bathe and assist Lenny in everything he did. It was drudgery for them and a complete zero in quality of life for him. They were performing Lenny's ADLs (activities of daily living), keeping him alive, but nothing they did was emotionally meaningful to him.

Looking back, I feel sad for those last years of Lenny's life. I was very fond of him. He was more of a father to me than my own father had been, and that's why it pains me that I didn't know then what I know now.

The lone impression his caregivers had of him was that of a shriveled, incompetent, occasionally cantankerous old man who was taking up valuable space on the planet.

If only they had known more about the man Lenny used to be, the big and small things that made him uniquely "Lenny," I'm certain his level of care would have significantly improved.

At my company, each client, or a family member, answers a set of questions called a social history (see some sample questions at the end of this chapter). The social history is important, because it helps every caregiver remember that each client is much more than their disease or condition.

"ADLs keep people alive. Meaningful activities give people a life worth living."

The social history is part of a holistic treatment approach. It allows for the creation of a customized treatment plan that includes activities meaningful to the person. We often say, "ADLs keep people alive. Meaningful activities give people a life worth living."

A good social history includes demographic information such as their family situation, marital status, personality traits and level of education.

A good social history also uncovers their values, religious beliefs, involvement in clubs and organizations, professional life and hobbies.

Caregivers can then leverage that information to enrich their treatment approach, with more significant conversation and activities.

Here were some facts about Lenny that a social history would have uncovered:

Lenny had been a cartographer during World War II and worked under General Dwight D. Eisenhower; he liked to eat a piece of bread at the end of every meal; he was a very good builder—he had added a top floor to a Cape Cod house he bought in the early years of his marriage, doing most of the work himself; he had a place for everything, and everything had its place; he was a golfer, gardener, amateur photographer, father and grandfather; and he was blessed with friends at the end of his life whom he had known since kindergarten.

Armed with those facts, caregivers could have fashioned activities that would have provided him a more suitable end-of-life experience instead of sticking him in front of the TV all day. For instance:

- Sorting and organizing coins or inexpensive pieces of hardware
- Building houses with Lincoln Logs
- Planting a little garden in a window box together that he could have helped tend

Lenny had lost much of his former self, but there were still remnants of interests that might have created a spark of joy or recognition in his world and better connected his past with his present.

He also might have been more cooperative had he sensed his caregivers' efforts to understand his needs and more inclined to work as a team with his caregivers.

Maybe you're not an official caregiver but are dealing with the deterioration of a loved one: Don't stop reading now!

Everything I've mentioned above can help considerably if you are interacting at any point with a loved one who is struggling with the ravages of aging or dementia—even someone you think you know very well.

We often assume we know the person who was in our life for years, but we forget a lot—and some facts we never knew.

Sometimes I address this topic in small groups of people who are caring for loved ones. Frequently they tell me that they can't imagine their loved one as anything but old and ailing. When they say that, it reminds me of the Clay Walker song, *Fore She Was Mama.*

The lyrics explain that when he was 10, he found a box of yearbooks, letters and photos in a closet and was shocked to see pictures of Mama "sittin' on a Harley, with some hairy hippie dude, drinkin', smokin', wearing a bikini in Tijuana, hip-high rose tattoo...."

So ask yourself this question: How much do you really know about your parents' youth—those days long before you were in the picture? Wouldn't it be fun and rewarding to find out before it's too late?

In my own family, my grandchildren think I fell out of a tree at 67 years old...that I've always had wrinkles and worn glasses. They don't know I had a real life before they came along. They can't imagine me young, dating their grandmother, holding hands with her, nervously kissing her for the first time and, even more nervously, meeting Lenny for the first time and being sized up by him.

They don't know that my preferred daily breakfast is Cheerios and a banana (to Irene's frustration), and that putting a bowl of shredded wheat in front of me will ruin my day.

This fact seems small, but imagine someone who loves Cheerios who is unable to fix their own breakfast being expected to eat shredded wheat. It could ruin their day too.

A social history helps you stop seeing a person as old. An old person is simply a young person in an old body. When your 90-year-old father looks in the mirror he doesn't see a 90-year-old man (although that's what I see sometimes, on a bad day). He sees the man he still believes himself to be, and the man he was.

A social history can remind you of who that person was, give you a glimpse into how that person sees himself or herself, and help you remember that they are a special individual, not a burden.

It can make the task of caregiving easier by giving you something to talk about and do with your loved one.

Another bonus is that you will have more patience. Being reminded of their social history, and the history the two of you have together, often reduces your annoyance when they ask you for the fourth time in five minutes what time it is. Why? Because there's more understanding, and you've strengthened your bond.

Strengthening your bond will build a bridge between generations, between the past and the present. You may learn things about your parent you never knew, or even hear stories about yourself you never heard or had forgotten.

If you're dealing with an aging parent, don't let another day go by without asking questions—lots of them. You may find yourself intrigued, surprised and gratified.

Even someone who has lost their short-term memory or their ability to care for themself hasn't lost their desire to feel important.

If a professional is taking care of your loved one, make sure the caregiver knows as much about him or her as possible, even if you have to conduct the social history for them.

Below is a sampling of questions caregivers and loved ones should ask. (These are here for your inspiration—our company social history form is much more comprehensive.)

I'm sure you can easily think of more:

What did you do for a living?

What jobs did you have before you settled on a career?

How did you meet Mother/Father?

What did you like about him/her?

What is your proudest achievement?

What's your favorite TV show?

What's your favorite music/entertainer?

What is your favorite charity? Why?

What clubs did/do you belong to?

(If in the military) What was it like being in the military?

What's your favorite holiday, and why?

What were your favorite pets?

Do you like to watch sports or did you play any sports?

What's your favorite family recipe?

What do you like to wear to bed?

What's your favorite food? What's your least favorite food?

You get the point. Use the space below to come up with more questions, then give it a try and see what comes from it.

_____

_____

_____

_____

_____

Falling Down The Donut Hole

Do You Get Coffee With That?
What You Should Know About The Changing Face Of Health Care

Every year in early October my mailbox starts filling up with beautiful brochures promising nirvana in the form of Medicare Advantage Plans (soon to be called Medicare Health Plans). With great fanfare, the plans' sponsors (overwhelmingly for-profit insurance companies) imply their plans are just as good as—maybe even better than—Medicare. Not only will I get medical care but they'll throw in a free gym membership, dental coverage, eye exams and a trip to Walt Disney World. (I'm joking about that last one.)

Frankly, this avalanche of plans is confusing as hell, but it's also very compelling. Why are these companies trying so hard to get me to "just say no" to conventional Medicare, which doesn't even offer me as much as a free toothbrush?

Why are these companies trying so hard to get me to "just say no" to conventional Medicare?

Because there's big money in managed care for them, and they're betting you can be lured with "perks" to sign up without reading too much of the fine print.

Navigating this swamp can make you feel like you're being tugged in both directions by a rope controlled by alligators.

Medicare is administered by the federal government and operates (with some exceptions I'll talk about further down) on the old "fee-for-service" business model: you choose any doctor who accepts Medicare, receive a service, and the doctor gets paid. Conventional Medicare gives the patient more medical care options but fewer "extras." It has fewer "bad surprises" but often has a higher premium than a Medicare Advantage Plan, which may have no cost to you at all! Navigating this swamp can make you feel like you're being tugged in both directions by a rope controlled by alligators.

Medicare Advantage Plans were formalized by Congress in 1997 as Medicare Part C, an alternative to Medicare. They are a symptom of the shift in medical care that has disrupted historical health care delivery, and will continue doing so.

These plans represent the new face of health care, and it's not always a pretty one for the patient.

In Medicare Advantage Plans, participating insurance companies receive a negotiated set fee every month for you (called capitation) in exchange for that company agreeing to take care of your medical needs, including hospitalization and, in many cases, prescription drugs. Plus those extras.

It sounds tantalizing, doesn't it, especially if it costs you less? However, it's crucial to understand how these plans work, because it's what you don't know that can get you into trouble. Medicare Advantage Plans advertise themselves as offering services similar to Medicare. But—and read this carefully—they...are...not...Medicare.

Never forget that there are no free rides in this space. These options may not be as good as they sound. For example, with most Medicare Advantage Plans you may be limited to a network of physicians.

In contrast to Medicare, many Medicare Advantage Plans don't travel well...their benefits are limited to one specific geographic location. Use an out-of-network physician and you may experience "sticker shock." If you do a lot of traveling, or if you were to develop a serious disease better treated at an out-of-area institution, you may find yourself with inadequate coverage. Medicare Advantage Plan companies aren't giving you benefits out of the goodness of their hearts. They are in business to make money, so they offer fringe benefits to entice you while incorporating aspects into the plan that may discourage utilization. (You don't see *that* in large print.) There's also an incentive for them to be stingy with services in order to fatten up their bottom line, giving you just enough care to keep you whole. You're being sold a "new and improved" health care plan, but what it's really doing is reducing utilization.

You pay a price for surrendering your health care to this sort of group: giving up some of your options. Unfortunately, many people only realize this once they require non-run-of-the-mill medical care, such as a specialist in another geographic area, and discover it's not covered. You need to make your choice of plan with a complete understanding of what you are buying.

(Side note: In 2017, I needed spinal fusion surgery. I live in Florida but was able to choose a top surgeon in New York to do my procedure because I am on conventional Medicare. Since I have a Medicare supplement as well, I didn't pay a dime. Had I had a Medicare Advantage Plan, I would have most likely been limited to surgeons in my area in Florida.)

I'm not saying that Medicare Advantage Plans are bad. For some, they are the best option because they are generally more affordable than Medicare Part A and Part B and associated supplements, with low or no monthly premiums. However, make yourself aware of the minuses as well as the plusses, and don't get reeled in by marketing hype.

Open enrollment

Open enrollment for Medicare, occurring every year typically between October 15 and December 7, is the calendar window when you can sign up for Medicare or a Medicare Advantage Plan, change your plan or add or subtract prescription drug coverage.

Managed care, growing fast these days, has the tacit support of the government because it reduces and stabilizes government expenditures on health care. I see this as the future of all health care coverage.

The plan you choose can impact your health care for the rest of your life.

Be very, very, very careful what you choose, especially when you first come onboard the Medicare train. The plan you choose can impact your health care for the rest of your life.

For "first timers" there are no medical questions and no "rating," meaning you will be accepted on whatever type of plan you choose, despite pre-existing conditions, at the regular premium rate.

Here's the problem: If you start with a Medicare Advantage Plan and a year later want to switch to conventional Medicare (or vice versa), you will be subject to medical questions and could have to pay a higher premium than you would have had you made it your original choice. Make sure the type of coverage you choose is the type of coverage you can live with long-term.

Refuse to be sold, no matter what you are buying. Don't make your decision based strictly on non-essential benefits. Think about what plan would work best for you in the worst-case scenario, and buy the best one you can afford.

Don't make the mistake of choosing a plan without knowing exactly what you are getting into. Don't be the victim of slick marketing.

Here are some questions AARP recommends you ask before deciding on a plan:

- How much will I have to pay for premiums, deductibles, doctor visits and hospital stays?

- Will I have to choose hospital and health care providers from a network?

- Will my doctors accept the coverage? If not, are there doctors near me who will?

- Will I need referrals to visit specialists?

- Will the plan cover me if I get sick while traveling in another state or out of the country?

- What will my prescription drugs cost?

- Are my drugs on the plan's drug list (or formulary)?

- Does the plan include the pharmacies I currently use?

- Can I get my prescriptions through the mail?

- Does the plan have a good quality rating?

Arthur Fitzwater, licensed insurance agent for eHealth-Medicare.com, explains that the specifics of each Medicare Advantage Plan depend on the particular insurance company offering it. As a result, your Medicare Advantage Plan may require higher out-of-pocket costs than original Medicare. Plan premiums, benefits, and copayments may change each year.

The insurance company may require you to follow strict rules to get coverage for certain services or health products, like getting referrals to see specialists. You may have to change your doctor or hospital to one within the Medicare Advantage Plan's network for coverage, or you may have to pay a higher fee.

Medicare Advantage Plans have annual contracts with Medicare and can choose not to renew their contract for the following year.

Advantages, according to Fitzwater, include:

- $0 premium from some plans.

- Additional benefits that are not covered by Part A and Part B of original Medicare, such as vision or dental coverage.

- A maximum out-of-pocket limit on how much you will spend on health costs each year. Once that limit is reached, you will pay nothing for covered services. Each Medicare Advantage Plan could have a different limit, and that amount may change each year. Medicare has no yearly limit.

You don't want to make decisions in a crisis.

You don't want to make decisions in a crisis. By the time you realize you made a mistake, your options are gone. We cannot protect against every calamity that befalls us, but we don't need to make the calamity worse by making an uninformed decision in advance.

My bottom line here: Be an educated consumer.

Drug plans

Whether you have Medicare or Medicare Advantage, you have the option to buy a prescription drug plan (some Medicare Advantage Plans include drug coverage). Be aware that what these plans cost, and what they cover, may change every year. You must scrutinize your drug plan annually.

Be aware of the details of your plan's particular "donut hole" which almost every prescription drug plan has: a gap in coverage during which you have to pay all costs out-of-pocket for your prescriptions up to a yearly limit.

Help!

It seems nearly impossible to navigate all the choices, but you're not alone in the woods. You can go to www.medicare.gov and look for a link to SHIP (State Health Insurance Assistance Program). SHIP has offices around the country and is there to help people navigate the murky waters of Medicare.

You may also be able to find an insurance agent in your area who specializes in Medicare but keep in mind he or she works on commission and "has a dog in the hunt."

Good-bye Mayberry

One sign of the changing face of health care is that doctor-patient relationships have changed radically over the years.

While you might still be able to find a doctor in a remote country town who accepts a chicken for a check-up, the payment system for 99.9% of us is vastly different than when we were children. So is the process of spending some one-on-one time with the doctor, getting the services we really need and follow-up care.

While there are plenty of compassionate "wanna-be Dr. Welbys" in the world, the system makes practicing medicine that way close to impossible. There are too many "money men" up the chain pulling the strings of the doctors who are tasked with providing health care for the lowest possible health care dollar.

Does the following situation sound familiar?

You show up on time for your doctor's appointment. The waiting room is jammed. You produce identification and insurance cards and fill out paperwork during the 47 minutes you're forced to cool your heels before being called in.

The Price is Right blaring in the background is adding to your annoyance.

Next, an underling sits at a small nook in the examining room, nose buried in a laptop computer, asking you a string of questions—most of which you already put down on paper during the previous 47 minutes. You spend four minutes with the doctor. You fork over your co-pay. You need to see a specialist, so you go home and wait for the referral and to have your needed service approved by a bean counter, battle with your insurance company...and on and on.

Chaos is now the norm

OK, I'll admit that this scenario and the problem it represents isn't new. The government and insurance companies have been trying to find something that works since the mid-1970s when health care costs began to skyrocket and HMOs debuted on the scene.

It's easy to end up not receiving the best medical care for your health, but rather the best medical care for the cost.

Being a patient these days is precarious business. It's easy to end up not receiving the best medical care for your health, but rather the best medical care for the cost.

As the face of health care rapidly evolves, the best way for the consumer not to get steamrolled in the process is to be educated about what's going on behind the scenes as well as to learn how to choose from the best of the shrinking options.

The fact that the government cannot figure out how to make health care work tells you how incredibly complex it is. Health care experts keep throwing ideas for payment against the wall, hoping something will stick, but nothing has stuck very well so far.

For example, Medicare has tried something called "bundling." (These figures are hypothetical, but the process is not.)

Let's say that Medicare agrees to pay your provider $20,000 for the entire process of a knee replacement, from your initial evaluation through your surgery to the last of your post-op rehab following replacement. The idea is to have a better continuity of care than if the patient had to deal on his own with doctors, pharmacies, rehab facilities, etc. Sounds good and simple, right?

Here's where the problem comes in: It's in the provider's best interest to spend less than $20,000 on your knee replacement bundle because—you guessed it—they get to keep the difference! Are they farming out the services you need to the lowest bidder?

Do they put you in a nursing home at $450 a day where you can have physical therapy two times daily or send a physical therapist to your home three times a week? Of course they don't want you to go to the nursing home, even though you are going to benefit from more therapy there.

To mitigate this influence, Medicare penalizes a hospital participating in bundled services that has what they consider too many re-admissions, supposedly counter-balancing the tendency to minimize services. It remains to be seen how this will shake out, but if you are someone needing a knee replacement in the meantime, you could be negatively impacted.

Interestingly, CMS (Medicare) is cutting back on the bundling initiative because it didn't seem to be working according to their business model. It may have brought costs down but increased re-admissions due to complications.

If you find yourself in this situation it will be up to you to be the squeaky wheel—to be the one who insists on the best level of care possible and to not accept anything less. Unfortunately, this self-advocate approach can put you at odds with your doctor—one of the disturbing trends of modern medicine.

Another cost initiative is Accountable Care Organizations (ACOs). These are groups of doctors, hospitals, and other health care providers who come together voluntarily to give coordinated high-quality care to their Medicare patients.

Health care providers today are being conditioned to do just the bare minimum of what is necessary for your well-being and to second-guess every health care expenditure. This includes the growing trend to provide people services at home rather than in rehab or hospital environments, even though the services in those facilities are likely to be more frequent and more beneficial than at-home care.

As yet there's no happy medium that reduces utilization and readmissions. Stay tuned. You're bound to be a part of whatever is next.

Just a few years ago doctors were prescribing tests that might have been unnecessary in order to protect themselves from lawsuits. This was part of fee-for-service, called "overutilization," and doctors and hospitals experienced no consequence for doing it. Today it's the opposite.

Doctors and hospitals get rewarded for underutilization.

Doctors and hospitals get rewarded for underutilization.

For Sale: Your Doctor's Practice
The independent physician is an anomaly these days. Doctors are losing the ability to practice medicine the way they want to, and this can impact your care.

The problem is that hospitals are buying all the medical practices in the area. It makes certain aspects of the doctor's life easier, such as no longer having to handle hiring and paying the bills. The downside, however, is that the doctors must answer to a "higher power" (and I don't mean God)–they must answer to the hospital's chief financial officer.

This arrangement ties your doctor's hands to a certain extent because if he or she isn't recommending a certain number of procedures or meeting some sort of income target, they could get booted out.

If I'm a cardiologist working for the hospital and they want me to put in seven stents each day and I only do six a day, the bosses won't be happy. The hospitals put pressure on doctors for volume.

All these restrictions have led to the rise of concierge medicine for people who can afford it. With concierge medicine you are no longer patient #416 but you are patient Scott Greenberg. The health care system in this country is becoming more and more bifurcated between the haves and the have-nots.

Unfortunately, the doctor's decision-making is influenced by some factors beyond just what's in the patient's best interest. This doesn't mean the doctor is bad or wants to do this. It's simply the world your doctor now inhabits. He or she must "stick with the program" of saving the employer money or risk being shown the door. This illustrates how patients' vision of healthcare and healthcare's vision of patients is not aligned anymore. We are rapidly heading toward being even more on opposite sides of the equation.

Electronic Medical Records
Are they good or are they bad? The answer is yes.

First the bad.

Electronic medical records have created a situation where your doctor spends more time looking at a computer screen in the examination room than looking at you.

A few years ago I went to the Cleveland Clinic once every 4-6 weeks for 18 months for a treatment by the same doctor. He was so busy typing that he almost never looked up at me during all those months, and I can guarantee you that if I had run into him outside of that office, he would have had no idea who I was. There was no personal touch whatsoever for me in that situation, and I felt more like a number.

One downside for the doctors is that electronic medical records place an unbelievable administrative burden on them as well as a financial burden.

Now for the good.

Electronic medical records are convenient because they allow your medical records to be instantaneously available to other health care providers, even those outside the doctor's group, as well as hospitals and nursing homes anywhere in the country—or the world for that matter.

This system worked in my favor when I used to go to the Mayo Clinic in Jacksonville, Florida, for an annual physical. The process involved seeing several specialists. After seeing the first doctor, I went to another floor of the hospital to see the next one, and the second doctor already had my notes from the first doctor.

Here's another example. A friend of mine had been hospitalized for a minor heart attack in 2003. Fourteen years later, when she became concerned about how she was feeling, she went to an urgent care center owned by the hospital system where she had been hospitalized. Although she was in a different city than the one in which she had been hospitalized, the doctor was able to pull up her EKG from 2003, compare it to the one in 2017 and assure her that her EKG was exactly like the old one. It put her mind to rest instantly.

Another advantage of electronic medical records is that they are generally typed, not hand-written. It's no myth about how bad most doctors' handwriting is. Typed notes are less likely to be misinterpreted. Information contained in these records also helps protect against mistakes or to prompt a "second opinion." Let's say you are taking a medication and your new doctor sees the name of that medication on your electronic record, and feels that your treatment needs to be revisited. It might improve the quality of your care, especially if you are on the wrong medication, don't need medication anymore or could benefit from a different medication.

In these ways, electronic medical records can be very helpful.

The bottom line here is that electronic medical records have the power to create a further divide between patients and doctors and the power to help. Love them or hate them, they're here to stay. I suggest you find a doctor who has figured out a way to balance the two.

Apps
Here's a change I think has more up-side than down-side, but it still results in less doctor-to-patient interaction.

Approximately one-third of people with smart phones have at least one health app. Besides doing such things as tracking fitness, other health issues can be monitored and sent wirelessly to the doctor or hospital. These include your EKG, glucose and performance of your pacemaker. This evolving technology is making it possible to share information regularly and directly with your doctor and keep an eye on chronic conditions. Ask your doctor about any available technology that can help you better partner with him or her.

What this all means
It doesn't bode well for the consumer that managed care is still unable to find its equilibrium. Every day the landscape

of the practice of medicine continues its dysfunctional trajectory toward even more chaos, all happening at warp speed.

Even if we'd like to, we can't halt the rapid changes going on in health care and technology. All we can do is stay abreast of the changes, make decisions based on fact rather than emotion, and never stop being an assertive advocate for our own health care.

Clearly, most of what's included here is factual. However, I must admit that some of my personal opinion has seeped in. As always, consult a true professional in the areas where you may have questions.

About The Author

Scott Greenberg is host of the weekly radio show "Oh My God, I'm Getting Older and So Is My Mom" on True Oldies Florida in Palm Beach and Martin Counties, Florida. He also serves as Chief Executive Officer of ComForcare Senior Services, a private duty non-medical home healthcare agency serving all of Palm Beach, Martin, St. Lucie and Indian River Counties in South Florida as well as in four counties in the Jacksonville area.

Scott is active in local healthcare initiatives and activities as a result of his business and his radio show. He is the Past President and currently serves as a board member of the Florida State Guardianship Association. Scott also serves as the Treasurer of the National Guardianship Association. In addition to those duties, he is an elected member of the Advisory Council of the Area Agency on Aging.

Prior to purchasing controlling interest in Palm Beach ComForcare, Scott was President of Curran and Connors, Inc., the nation's largest designer of corporate annual reports. He grew Curran & Connors, Inc. from a small, one studio design firm into 16 offices, including four design studios across the United States. During his tenure, the firm was twice named one of Long Island's 25 fastest-growing companies by KPMG, one of the largest professional services companies in the world; and Small Business of the Year by the Hauppauge Industrial Association. Scott was a finalist in Ernst & Young's Entrepreneur of the Year program;

and was one of only six businessmen in the New York metropolitan area selected to judge Arthur Andersen's Best Practices Competition for three consecutive years.

Scott is often called on to speak on topics of importance to various audiences. A full list of his speaking venues and topics can be seen on the Speaking Engagements tab of his website:
www.omgimgettingolderandsoismymom.com

Scott resides in Jupiter, Florida, with his wife, Irene.

Scott welcomes your outreach and can be reached directly (see below). He is available to speak to your group. Below is his contact information:

Snail mail:
Scott Greenberg
333, LLC
9121 N. Military Trail, Suite 216
Palm Beach Gardens, FL 33410

E-mail:
slg123@comcast.net

Phone:
(561) 706-5157

Endorsements

As a physician, knowing that Scott Greenberg and his team are out there helping to care for our most frail, elderly patients gives me great comfort. Scott is a successful entrepreneur with a kind-hearted soul. In a word, Scott is a mensch!

Stuart J. Bagatell, MD, FACP

Scott Greenberg continues to apply passion and great energy to help improve the future for aging baby-boomers and elderly throughout his community. His laser like focus and no-nonsense approach is truly remarkable and an inspiration for others to model.

Mark Armstrong
ComForcare Senior Services

Having had the pleasure of knowing Scott Greenberg personally and professionally, I feel I must weigh in. In the world of aging, I come across all kinds of people who work in this field, but there are two kinds that stand out in my mind: those who mainly work for the paycheck, and those who care more about the seniors they serve. Scott Greenberg exemplifies the latter in more ways than one. He knows how difficult it is for families emotionally and financially when it comes to finding help for their aging loved ones. He knows how confusing it can be for the families to negotiate their way around the ins and outs of this fast-growing field. If you're looking for Scott's heart, you'll find it in his work...and it shows in the hours he invests as he's always available when you need him. You see, of the two types of workers I mentioned, no matter how committed and hard-

working these caregivers are, there can be an ocean of difference in how they give care. Scott Greenberg is the very definition of "caring"...especially when it comes to seniors.

Jaime Estremera-Fitzgerald
Chief Executive Officer
Area Agency on Aging/Your Aging & Disability Resource Center

Scott Greenberg has done it again. Scott's no-nonsense, practical and entertaining approach on aging issues continues in this must read for everyone concerned about a loved one's later years as well as their own. My clients and their families praise the value of the information Scott provides with his extensive experience and sense of humor.

Michelle Hollister
Elder Law Attorney

When Scott Greenberg first wrote, "Oh My God I'm Getting Older and So Is My Mom," I had the distinct pleasure of writing an endorsement that personified his background leading up to writing the book. Since that time, Scott has become more involved in family caregiving seminars and support groups. Further, his extensive knowledge of home health care, guardianship and his unique ability to put the "bigger picture" of aging and caring in America together with a keen understanding of people's attitudes, wants and needs make him an author/observer of incredible depth. With the addition of four new chapters and a review and updating of the previous content, the book now creates an even more outstanding resource and perspective for the reader. Combined with his wisdom and unique sense of humor, this new edition is still a "must read" as it adds and clarifies what he has learned in the years since the first edition. As an industry "change agent" he has accomplished what he has set out to do with this book.

David Levy, JD, CCE
Gerontologist and author of "The Family Caregiver Manual"

Through the years, I have seen the care, dedication, compassion and patience Scott offers for those who need guidance and support. His knowledge and skills leave no question as to his ethical guidelines and professional standards of practice. I am proud to call Scott Greenberg a friend and mentor. Thank you for the hard work and outstanding efforts you put into everything you do!

Karen Greene
Nurse Care Manager & National Certified Guardian
Hired Hearts, Inc., President/CEO
Florida State Guardianship Association, President

Scott Greenberg has a passionate expertise for the services he provides his clients and their families. He and his team give the highest level of support to people with special needs, that often times arise in the course of our general lives. Through their care, the quality of the lives of the patient, and the families, are enhanced.

Richard A. Levine MD, FACP

Getting older is not for the faint of heart. Watching your parents age is even scarier. Scott Greenberg's book doesn't take the stress and fear of the experience away, but it talks about it all in a thoughtful and often humorous way that makes the scariness of it all just a little easier to take. A must read for anyone with aging parents and a desire to think ahead to what is to come.

Mitchell I. Kitroser, Esq.
Kitroser & Associates